College Heights Church
710 College St. Rd.
Elizabethtown, KY 42701

That's Good News

Shane L. Bishop

That's Good News

How to Overcome
Your Fear and Evangelize

invite
PRESS
Plano, Texas

THAT'S GOOD NEWS: HOW TO OVERCOME YOUR FEAR AND EVANGELIZE
Copyright 2023 by Shane L. Bishop

All rights reserved.

This book is printed on acid-free, elemental chlorine-free paper.

Paperback: 978-1-953495-55-6; eBook: 978-1-953495-56-3

23 24 25 26 27 28 29 30 31 32—10 9 8 7 6 5 4 3 2 1

MANUFACTURED IN THE UNITED STATES OF AMERICA

Contents

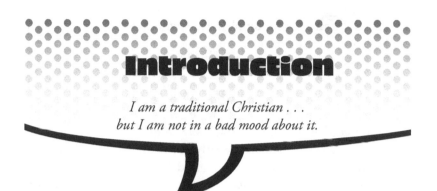

Introduction

I am a traditional Christian . . .
but I am not in a bad mood about it.

Evangelism is sharing the message of Jesus Christ under the influence of the Holy Spirit. Does this charge seem daunting? It doesn't have to be.

In fact, evangelism is so aligned with the will of God that it is hard to mess up, regardless of how badly you do it. I know lots of people who received Christ through hellfire, "in your face," propositional approaches to evangelism, but I have never met anyone who found Jesus through not having the Gospel shared with them at all. Let's face it, we all know evangelism is the "reproductive system" of Christianity; it is how people are invited to know Jesus. The more evangelism, the more Christians. We equally know that the very concept of evangelism intimidates more Christians every day. The less evangelism, the fewer Christians. This is problematic by any measure.

Why are we intimidated?

- Perhaps we have forgotten that the Gospel is good news.

- Perhaps we have lost clarity concerning our own beliefs.

- Perhaps we fear rejection and pushback.

- Perhaps we fear we will do more harm than good if we share our faith.

- Perhaps we have no idea how to share our faith.

Let me give it to you straight; we are called by God and empowered by the Holy Spirit to be effective evangelists for Christ. God is fully capable of blessing and multiplying any witness we offer . . . no matter how messed up it may be.

Harold
• • • • •

I am convinced that the only way to get evangelism wrong is not to evangelize. An encounter early in my ministry taught me this lesson very well. I encountered Harold in the mid-1990s when I served as a United Methodist pastor in a small Illinois town, and Robert Schuller was one of the most famous television preachers in the country.

Harold was somewhere between eighty and 200 years old. He had killed people in World War II and then worked thirty years in a condom factory before retiring to a modest pension. These two life events misshaped his personality like an irregular pair of shoes eventually deform the feet. Harold was my neighbor. I walked by his yellow mobile home each day on my way to and from the parsonage of the Sumner United Methodist Church. I was warned about Harold: "He is a recalcitrant and curmudgeon, an old man who doesn't like anybody but especially hates preachers."

Harold sat outside his metallic front door on a small, wooden porch in good weather, and I cheerfully greeted him every morning and evening. He raised a hand but never spoke. This was our routine, and we did it every day. One day, he said, "I heard you like sweet tea." It was the first time he had spoken to me. I replied, "That is not exactly right; I like fresh brewed, southern sweet tea where the sugar is melted in while the water is hot." He said, "I can make tea like that. Stop by sometime." I told him I would and walked on to work. (We had been at this for three years; I didn't want to appear easy.) A couple of weeks later I paid Harold a call (preachers used to do such things), and he brought me a mason jar filled with better than average sweet tea. Once settled in, Harold talked about WWII. I had the strong feeling he had never spoken about these things to anyone before. We were on holy ground. He spoke of young men who didn't return home; he called them by name. He described the face of a German sniper he had shot out of a tree and the horror of removing the soldier's helmet as her blond hair flowed out. He described the circumstances resulting in two Purple Hearts and watching his own surgery being performed in the chandelier above him in a mansion turned field hospital.

Harold also spoke of how badly the church had hurt him as a young man. Upon returning from the war, he had impregnated his ultra-religious girlfriend; both of them were summarily ostracized by her family and by her congregation. He said, "We had nowhere to turn. It destroyed her life." He cried like a baby through most of it. And then something happened; he shut off the tears, said he didn't need me or my church, and I was curtly dismissed. I left a half glass of sweet tea on his table wondering what had just happened. After that our relationship returned to its previous state for a year or so, but I thought a lot about Harold.

One night, his wife Edna called me in the early morning hours in a panic: "I can't control Harold. He is having seizures, and the ambulance isn't here. Can you come and help me?" When I arrived, Harold was in the restroom with his eyes rolled back into his head, pants hanging at his ankles, and was urinating all over the place as he convulsed against the wall. I took a deep breath, waded in, and helped Edna. All the while Harold was crying out to God, "God, if you will let me live, I will give my life to you."

The ambulance finally arrived. The paramedics strapped Harold to a board and took off for Evansville. I went home and took a long, really, hot shower, threw my clothes in the washing machine, and went to bed. A couple of days later, I drove the hour and a half to Evansville and entered Harold's hospital room. He was in pretty bad shape, but that did not keep him from scowling and physically turning away from me. I sat down. We sat in silence for several minutes. When Harold determined that I wasn't going to leave, he whispered over the oxygen tank, "You heard me didn't you? I meant what I said about giving my life to God; but you won't be seeing me in your church. I am going to watch Robert Schuller on television." For some reason, that one really hacked me off, and I got about two inches from the tube up Harold's nose and whispered in his ear, "I have a great idea for you, Harold. The next time you are having seizures, can't control yourself in the toilet, and are about three-quarter's nuts, why don't you have Edna give Robert Schuller a call? See if he will get out of bed in California, fly to Sumner, and come over to your house in the middle of night. See if he will help your wife care for you and endure your unique physiological rendition of, "Showers of Blessing," all over his sweatshirt?" I slammed the hospital door behind me and left. It occurred to me this was possibly not a textbook example of pastoral care.

Harold was released the next week, and though he never said a single thing about our hospital conversation, he attended church the next Sunday and never missed another worship service at the Sumner United Methodist Church. He sat about midway back and to my right. Edna sat next to him beaming. Harold was alive and in church. Her prayers had been answered!

About a year later, I received another call from Edna. Harold was dead in his Lay-Z-Boy, and she wondered if I would stop by and sit with her until the county coroner arrived. There we sat in three chairs in the tiny living room: Edna, Harold, and me. Edna asked if I wanted a glass of tea. I said, "Sure." She handed me a glass and began to cry, "I don't exactly know what you said to Harold in the hospital room, but it changed his life. He found Jesus." A bit perplexed, I inquired, "Did Harold say anything at all about our conversation?" Edna replied, "Not really. He just said you were the first preacher who ever explained things to him in a way he could understand."

I did almost everything wrong. I certainly would not have made my pastoral care professors at Candler School of Theology proud. Apart from remaining conscious throughout the entire encounter, I doubt I did anything right at all. I did, however, learn something. God can work even through a hospital call that was a technical disaster. When it comes to evangelism, it appears that God can bless anything, except nothing.

This is a book about giving God something to bless.

Both Sides of the Bullhorn

I cut my evangelistic teeth doing street ministry with No Greater Love Ministries (NGL) long before I became a pastor. My father,

Fred Bishop, founded NGL as a "Men's Evangelistic Ministry" in 1976. You might say evangelism is our "family business." Dad has taken thousands of men to high density and historically rowdy events like the street parties surrounding the New Orleans Mardi Gras, Indianapolis 500, and Kentucky Derby for over fifty years. The general idea is to provide training in faith-sharing techniques, wade into the middle of the scrum, boldly proclaim Christ, and then process what you experienced in small groups once you get back to camp. On these faith-sharing trips, men learn to share a testimony, street preach, do clown ministry, pass out Gospel tracts, and conduct a Jesus march. They are thrown into volatile situations "over their heads," and they must learn to rely on the Holy Spirit to see them through. It is an evangelism boot camp. For NGL, street evangelism is the means by which the ends of spiritually equipping men for evangelism is powerfully accomplished. Through NGL, I learned that evangelism cuts both ways; it reaches both the evangelist and the one being evangelized. Street ministry may not be for everyone, but I have seen innumerable lives impacted on "both sides of the bullhorn" over the decades. On these evangelistic excursions, men are equipped with evangelistic skills they can take back home and implement in their own communities and churches.

Twice Back at You
• • • • • • • • • • •

On the streets, you are playing an *away* game where Satan always has home field advantage. It is here that immovable objects and irresistible forces collide in the spirit world. It is here that miracles occur. There will always be something raw, unfiltered, and honest for me about street evangelism. Evangelism in the context of street ministry is straight up spiritual warfare.

Growing up the son of a Bible smuggler, pastor, and evangelist, I have had the opportunity to meet many colorful folks. Few were more interesting than Phil. Phil is a deep Southern Illinois native and a painter by trade. He does prison and deliverance ministry and has led hundreds of people to Christ each year for decades. He is a soul-winning machine. Phil's life is dedicated to speaking words of healing, deliverance, or salvation. It is literally all he talks about.

One year, on the Mardi Gras trip, a practitioner of voodoo locked in on Phil just outside Jackson Square in New Orleans. He was a filthy, diminutive, and wiry guy with dreadlocks who had nothing on but dirty shorts and some kind of feather thing on his head. His body and face were all tatted up with various and sundry devil stuff. He had nothing in his hand but a piece of sidewalk chalk. Something about Phil drove this guy even more crazy than he already was, and he began to stalk Phil. He finally approached and drew a chalk circle around Phil, began to speak unintelligible hexes, delivered dark curses, and literally danced around the circle. All the while Phil stood motionless, completely unintimidated, smiling slightly, and watching with sheer amusement. When the incantation was complete, the witch doctor defiantly locked eyes with Phil, probably expecting him to die on the spot.

Phil didn't die. In fact, he didn't even blink. Still locked in a stare down, Phil spoke but four words in a Southern Illinois drawl, "Twice back at you." The little voodoo man looked as if a knife had been driven into his soul. He contorted, screamed violently, and disappeared into the crowd at a full sprint.

Final Score:

Phil: 1

Voodoo Man: 0

Evangelism for *Regular* People
• • • • • • • • • • • • • • • • • • •

If you are thinking that street evangelism doesn't seem cut out for *regular* people, you are probably right. Perhaps the very idea of this kind of evangelism is what intimidates so many Christians. Let's face it; taking people on a mission work trip is a far easier sell than sharing faith with the hostile hoards. For the past four decades, evangelism has been a major part of my pastoral ministry, and unlike my early years, the vast majority has been conducted in the crucible of the local church. My evangelistic efforts these days primarily center upon all-church outreaches and equipping *regular* people to share faith with their family, friends, co workers, and neighbors. Such evangelistic techniques are neither forced nor manufactured, but they do take planning and intentionality. I will share the most effective of these methods with you in the chapters to come. We will also discuss some methods of doing all-church evangelism. There may not be as many exciting stories with this kind of evangelism, but the majority of the people I have seen come to Jesus and follow him into discipleship have done so in the context of the local church.

Street ministry is *propositional* evangelism aimed at reaching strangers in a one-time encounter. It is an away game. You will never see these people again. You can go right at it. When people respond, you hope they connect to a local church when they get home.

Church ministry is *relational* evangelism aimed at reaching people you know in the context of community. It is a home game. These are your family, friends, and neighbors. It requires a softer touch. When people respond, a church is awaiting them with open arms.

Both propositional and relational evangelism are needed. For our purposes, we will focus upon the latter. In this book, I hope to challenge the way we think about evangelism, help you overcome the intimidation factor, and widen our collective imaginations as to how *regular* people can effectively reach others for Jesus.

Hellfire and Salvation

Jesus called Peter and Andrew to be "fishers of men," and that calling is extended to all who answer Christ's call to become disciples of Jesus. Many of the twelve disciples were commercial fishermen on the Sea of Galilee. They caught fish or they starved. If you couldn't catch fish in one place, you went to another. If you couldn't catch fish with one technique, you shifted to another. There were no excuses. It was that simple. This "get it done gear" was the mentality Jesus was looking for in his inner core. It is a mentality he is still looking for today. We don't need to rethink what it means to be a "people fisher" but we need to constantly be evaluating our methods of attracting the fish.

Most Christians I knew as a child were products of a Christian home. They received Christ at a young age, were baptized, and were reared in the nurture of the church. How was a profession of faith achieved so soon? Hellfire and salvation.

I was saved when I was seven. We were holding a revival at Oak Wood Baptist Church in Ft. Worth, Texas, and I walked down the aisle during the invitation, somewhere between the fortieth and forty-first verse of "Just as I Am." At that altar, I repented of my dastardly ways, prayed to receive Christ, and was summarily baptized. It is a time I remember most warmly, as I truly felt God reaching to me. I responded to the best of my childhood ability. I am so glad my parents encouraged me. You can say what you want about childhood conversions, but there is no doubt in my mind that I was saved when I was seven.

A couple of years later, I was just beginning my Sunday school career at the Oak Grove Baptist Church north of Pinckneyville, Illinois. We often participated in a corporate exercise called "When, Where, and Why." The idea was simple; all the elementary-school aged kids got into a circle, and when our turn came around, we were to answer the following three questions: When did you receive Jesus? Where were you when your received Jesus? Why did you receive Jesus? The *When* responses were all recent, after all we were just kids and no one had been a Christian for very long. The *Where* responses varied, but for the most part they happened at church, home, or at camp. However, the *Why* was always exactly the same. Every Baptist kid I knew in the early 1970s got saved because he or she didn't want to go to hell. Let me tell you right now, *no one* wanted to go to hell.

When I was growing up, hell received a lot of attention in church. In addition to sermons about hell, there were Sunday school lessons about hell, songs about hell, and movies about hell. The scariest movie of them all, *The Burning Hell*, was released in 1974 and starred a horn-rimmed Baptist preacher from Mississippi named Estus W. Pirkle. While it didn't win any Oscars, it was plenty horrifying to pre teens from the Hooterville/Pixley Circuit, and if you had some hell in you during the opening scene, it was scared out of you by the final credits.

If such means were crude evangelism tools, they were certainly effective. Did I mention that I got saved when I was seven years old? I also got saved when I was eight, nine, nine and a half, ten, twelve, and twice when I was thirteen.

I have thought about all of this over the years, and here is my conclusion: I am grateful that people shared Jesus with me.

I once heard a street preacher shout to a crowd, "Get your life insurance here!" That was the old bait. We were headed to hell and, by receiving Christ into our lives, our eternal address would now be heaven. Since life is uncertain, the sooner you make the move, the better! Such evangelistic techniques were highly effective but were predicated upon shared assumptions about the afterlife from a Christian perspective. To say such assumptions are not as widely held in our *post-Christian* culture as they were when I was a child would be an understatement. These basic assumptions are not even held in many churches today.

We don't need to compromise our message of eternal salvation made possible by the life, death, and resurrection of Jesus Christ. The message is alive and well. We don't need to stop sharing our faith. The Great Commission hasn't changed, and the Holy Spirit is still empowering witnesses on one hand and drawing unbelievers toward Jesus on the other. Our evangelistic task today is to hold fast to our message of the forgiveness of sin and eternal salvation through faith in Christ but be creative with how we communicate that message. Churches who are flexible with their message and inflexible with their methods are on the endangered species list if they are not extinct already. Churches who are inflexible on theology but creative with methodology will have a future and a hope.

Switching Methodology
• • • • • • • • • • • • • •

I am not a good or patient fisherman (the two are interrelated). Every time I have a reel in my hands, I suspect this is *the* day all the fish on the planet have finally figured things out. This is the point when I usually go home, but bailing on the day doesn't even cross the mind of real anglers. Have you ever gone fishing with an experienced bass fisherman in a boat? The tackle box is filled with different lures, all demanding a different technique for maximum effectiveness. Unlike bad fishermen, these people don't sit all day in one spot, baking in UV rays and futility; they keep switching lures and keep moving until they find somewhere the fish are biting. If that doesn't work, they try it all over again the next day. What if we changed our evangelistic methodology?

Old Method: Avoid eternal hell.

New Method: Receive a life filled with peace, purpose, power, and passion.

- What if personal conversion was touted as a completely different way to live than the template offered by this world?

- What if the prospect of becoming a disciple of Christ was presented as edgy, risky, and thoroughly countercultural?

- What if we presented Christian discipleship as a life brimming with peace, power, passion, and purpose that is so all-consuming that physical death isn't even a speed bump?

If we can affect a bait change, might we then proclaim that, in Christ, we can embrace a life filled with faith, hope, and love, a life where we trade despair for hope, confusion for clarity, and meaninglessness for purpose?

Life in Christ is the greatest trade of all time!

Ready for the bonus? This life isn't just for now. It is forever!

Reclaiming the Good News

Mainstream western culture deems orthodox Christians as haters, evangelism of any kind as hostile, and the words of Jesus, "I am the way, the truth, and the life. No one comes to the Father except through me," (John 14:6 NIV)," as exclusive. They have not only rejected the terms of discipleship but have vilified them. Rather than push back on the false narrative, many Christians have capitulated entirely. This quickly relegates expressions of faith to safe spaces like church, assuming your church is a safe place. It should not be surprising that many tentative believers have *withdrawn* their Christian witness from the public square altogether for fear of cultural pushback. They don't initially change what they believe but are frightened into internalizing faith and witness. Because of this, faith begins to atrophy and will eventually die. The justification for this is "do no harm," which has become more central in the belief system of many tepid Christians than the Bible itself. The reality is that, by our capitulation, we allow the demonic agenda of Satan to be shoved down the throats of our family, friends, and neighbors. And we allow it without offering those who are looking for another path an opportunity to hear the Good News of Christ. More people are ready to hear a compelling Gospel message than there are Christians willing to proclaim it. God forbid that our collective witness be silenced for fear of setting someone off on social media, getting a bit of pushback at work, or losing *friends* (who are happy to share their thoughts but want no part of yours).

The Abdication of Evangelism (for Any Reason) Is Not a Christian Option

I believe you can be a consistent and effective witness in a culture that desperately needs Christ on one hand and is increasingly hostile to Christianity on the other. It won't be easy, but it can be done. The whole of Christianity is an upstream walk against the current of this fallen world.

Are you ready to push against the current?

I am!

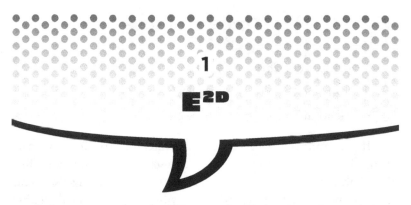

1

E²D

It is no secret that the Western church has been in precipitous decline for decades. In fact, we are not just in decline, we are dying. The reasons are legion, but I do not consider the presenting issues of non stop scandals, human sexuality debates, and the implosion of the mainline denominations to be the sole culprits. The bottom line has more to do with mathematics than theology. We are not converting enough new Christians to replace those who are dying. While it is true that you reap what you sow, you don't reap today what you sow today. We are reaping today what we sowed (or more correctly, failed to sow) yesterday. Today's church is experiencing the catastrophic results of yesterday's de-emphasis upon evangelism. We have sparse crops because, decade after decade, we have put far too few seeds in the ground, and we seem to be sowing fewer seeds all the time. If we are to experience different outcomes, we need new inputs.

Over the past twenty-five years, I have seen our congregation grow from about two hundred each week in worship to well over 2,000 in live attendance. Our growth and commitment to evangelism has been relentless, often recognized, and well chronicled. Our baseline evangelism strategy is, "You invite people to church, and we will treat them well and tell them about Jesus once they get here." The formula has proven effective. For a church to grow or to turn things around, you have to do three things: make new Christians, turn new Christians into disciples, and send disciples out to make new Christians.

Three Things
• • • • • • • • •

1. Make new Christians.

2. Turn new Christians into disciples.

3. Send disciples out to make new Christians.

If you want the "secret sauce" of church growth, it is two parts evangelism to one part discipleship. The scientific formula for Christian vitality is E^{2D}. Trying to grow a church without evangelism is like trying to make water (H^2O) without hydrogen. It can't be done. Hydrogen is two-thirds of the recipe! You can't grow a church without evangelism, and doubling up on other things won't help. Evangelism is the reproductive system of the body of Christ. Without an understanding of it, a strategy for it, and excitement around it, every existing church is in a death cycle whether the numbers show it or not. Most of us intuitively know that we must reload evangelism before we become extinct, but how do you get an object at rest into motion?

Let's see what the most effective evangelist in the history of the world had to say. Paul had every confidence that new Christians and the new churches he had planted could offer a credible and attractive witness to his jagged, manic, and hostile world. How to do this is outlined in his prison letter written to his protégé Timothy. As of this writing, Paul is incarcerated for no other reason than for doing God's work, being effective in evangelism, and getting on Rome's last nerve. He writes to an expanding but persecuted church to remind them of the imperative of continuing to share the faith. Paul's message provides us a firm place to stand today.

> This is why I remind you to fan into flames the spiritual gift God gave you when I laid my hands on you. For God has not given us a spirit of fear and timidity, but of power, love, and self-discipline.
>
> So never be ashamed to tell others about our Lord. And don't be ashamed of me, either, even though I'm in prison for him. With the strength God gives you, be ready to suffer with me for the sake of the Good News.
>
> *—2 Timothy 1:6-8*

We live in an historical time defined by mania. People are radiating at high frequencies. *Manic* derives from a Greek word meaning "inclined to madness." Synonyms include *anxious, hysterical, worried, demonic, unhinged, unbalanced,* and *feverish.* That all seems about right. To greater or lesser extents, we all feel the pull of the manic tide in this age of cultural wars, polarizing politics, racial division, economic disparity, terrorism, global intrigue, and information-selling, all kept at a frenzied pitch by people who have discovered there is good money in mania. But Christians are anything but helpless. Let's explore what it means to thrive and reproduce as Christian people in a manic world.

Verse 6. Fan into flames the spiritual gift God gave you.

Many years ago, a frustrated parishioner was airing his angst concerning congregational apathy during a Sunday evening testimony time. He said, "God wants to move here but most of you people can't experience it because your wood is all wet." I think he was on to something. We live in a cabin in the woods and burn lots of fires in cool weather. Wet wood doesn't burn very well.

May I get personal? Are you on fire for Jesus, or is your wood all wet? Did you used to love God more than you do right now? Do you remember a time when you truly felt passion for seeing people come to Jesus? Fan into flames the spiritual gift God gave you!

Verse 7. For God has not given us a spirit of fear and timidity.

If it were easy to evangelize, most every church in America would be thriving. Few churches in America are thriving. Tapping back into E^{2D}, I think most churches are reasonably comfortable on the one-part discipleship side and next to non existent on the two-parts evangelism side. Why? We are fearful and timid. That is the bad news. The good news is that, to aid us in our evangelistic mission, God has given us three powerful spiritual weapons: power, love, and self-discipline.

Three Spiritual Weapons
• • • • • • • • • • • • • • • •

1. Power: You are capable of being an influential witness.

Power is the supernatural ability to live into what God asks of us. God will never ask us to do what God has not empowered us to do. God has called us to be witnesses in the Great Commission and empowered us to be witnesses at Pentecost. The power is readily available. A failure to share faith is a power outage.

2. Love: You are capable of being an effective witness.

Love is the supernatural disposition God gives his children toward the world. First John 4:20 says, if we say we love God but hate people, we are liars and we deceive ourselves. Unconditional love does not require unconditional approval but it does require wanting the best for the souls of all people. A failure to share faith is a failure to love.

3. Self-discipline: You are capable of being a consistent witness.

The KJV translates this Greek concept, "a sound mind" rather than self-discipline. A sound mind here would mean seeing things God's way and not the world's way. It is to put on "the mind of Christ." Like eating clean and working out, evangelism will never be intuitive to our fallen nature. Evangelism is a discipline.

Verse 8. "Never be ashamed to tell others about our Lord." Give me the strength to suffer for the proclamation of the Good News.

Being a witness for Christ may cost us something, but none of us is likely to give our lives for the faith. Over the past decades, significant parts of the church have departed from biblical authority, clear moral teaching, and orthodox understandings of salvation, the afterlife, and sin. Those of us who have held firm to the historic faith and have attempted to speak the truth in love have done so in a time when many consider biblical truth to be hateful. I suspect we have all taken our proverbial lumps. We all want to be popular, particularly those of us who used to be. But our bruised egos and folks chipping at us on Facebook is not persecution, not compared to the early church. If you can *unfriend* or *block* someone with a click, you are not being persecuted. Every time I start feeling sorry for myself about how much some don't appreciate my clear stand for orthodox Christianity and for the Bible, God says, "Stop it. You are embarrassing yourself. Do you have any idea the price my followers have paid for their faith over the centuries? Now stop dripping weak sauce on holy ground. Cowboy up and crack at it!"

Our stand for Jesus won't cost us much, but failing to share the true faith in these times could cost an unbeliever everything.

For me, the evangelism imperative comes down to three simple questions: (1) Do you trust the testimony of the Bible? (2) Do you love Jesus enough to share him with people? (3) Do you love people enough to share Jesus with them?

Three Questions

1. "Do you trust the testimony of the Bible?"
2. "Do you love Jesus enough to share him with people?"
3. "Do you love people enough to share Jesus with them?"

If our answer to these three questions is affirmative, we have no choice but to evangelize. How will these evangelistic efforts go? It can get jagged. Though evangelism is difficult to mess up in a macro sense, it doesn't mean things can't go a bit off the rails in a micro sense. You have to be persistent and keep a sense of humor.

A Taste of the Gospel

I attended a No Greater Love Ministries evangelistic outreach to the Kentucky Derby in the mid-1980s. The idea was that, as the crowds entered Churchill Downs, we would hoist big Gospel signs, hand out Gospel tracts, and sing to them, and then do the same as they exited. I was with a small group working the front gate when a friend handed a Gospel tract called "The Big Question" to a drunk and shirtless man in his late twenties. This guy was sporting a few bad tattoos (I hope he wasn't charged full price) in the days before everyone had tattoos. He had a wild look in his eye. Clearly, we had his attention.

The young man took the tract, stared us down, and without giving the tract a glance, summarily shoved it in his mouth. It seemed to be going well for him at first, but as he chewed and began to experience the full flavor of dyed paper and black ink in his mouth and the accompanying dryness, he slowed down. A decent-sized crowd watched as he continued to chew. We were all wondering if the guy could get the tract down. He was starting to look like those guys do on the Food Channel when they are three-quarters of the way through a ten-pound hamburger. The dude looked sick. It was clear to me that this was the best witnessing trip in which I had ever participated.

Right when I would have bet that he was going to spit the whole thing out and abort mission, he reached deeply within, conjured up some alcohol infused spit, and, with a Herculean effort, swallowed. You could literally feel it going down. Upon the accomplishment of this feat (which was admittedly impressive), he zoned in and looked at me defiantly with anger in his eyes. The next move was going to be mine. I looked him straight in the eyes, smiled, and said, "Now it's going to be like two or three days before you can read that tract."

Jagged.

How did that evangelistic encounter turn out? I have no idea, but I doubt the guy read *that* tract.

And on that note, we *can* do this evangelism thing!

Let's have prayer together and then "crack on!"

Prayer
• • • •

Almighty God, would you fan our flickering faith into a mighty flame?

6

Would you take away our fear and timidity
    and fill us with power, love, and self-discipline?
Empower us to share your Good News with others.
Help us to never, never be ashamed,
    and grant us the willingness to suffer
    for the proclamation of your Good News!
We pray in the strong name of Jesus.
Amen!

2
What Makes the Good News Good?

In a culture that views theology through a political lens, words can quickly lose their meaning. A common political technique is to take a word with which most people are familiar but can't exactly define, artificially infuse it with every bad thing, and use the word as if that is what it meant all along. It is word robbery. I remember well my days as a young United Methodist pastor. People were coming to Jesus for the first time but were not necessarily familiar with church. The Apostles, Creed was problematic for many of them because of its historical use of the world *catholic*. I would explain that *catholic* predated the Roman Catholic church and meant "universal." When they asked why we didn't change it to *universal*, I informed them that despite the official asterisk, I had no intention of giving a perfectly good word away. *Catholic* it was.

Few Christian words have been more politicized in recent years than the word *evangelical*. Since *evangel* is the root (and a full 70 percent) of the word *evangelism*, let's deal with it simply and early. *Evangel* unites the Gospel with the ministry of a messenger. The Greek word *angelos*, translated "angel," can be a heavenly or an earthly being. What make one an angel is not your personal point of origin but the origin of your message. Angels bring messages from God to people. *Evangel* means "a messenger of Good News"; *ism* puts it into motion. Once again, I have no intention of giving a perfectly good word away. *Evangelism* it is!

8

The *E-Word*
● ● ● ● ● ● ● ●

For many years in mainline circles, evangelism was called the *E-Word*. It seemed most ironic to me that the one thing these formal clusters of dying clergy and churches most needed was deemed so taboo that people wouldn't even say the word. It was as if organized Christianity had suddenly forgotten that the Gospel is good news.

What Is the Gospel?
● ● ● ● ● ● ● ● ● ● ● ● ●

First-century Christians referred to the Gospel as "Good News." As transmitters of this Good News, they felt they were bringing something positive and desirable to people. That is why they were so excited about sharing it. Everyone wants to share good news! From their theological perspective, humanity was created to be in absolute unity with God (Creation) and original sin (The Fall) had ruined the whole thing. Humanity now had a terminal soul disease called *sin*, and the Gospel offered an eternal fix made possible by the life, death, and resurrection of Jesus. They also believed that the Good News was anchored in immutable truth. The Gospel was not a flighty or expedient "patch for a bug." It was rooted in the Old Testament itself. The Good News wasn't just true. It was truer than true.

Gospel Truth
● ● ● ● ● ● ● ●

I love the axiom called the "Gospel Truth." This refers to truth devoid of even a hint of untruth. This is difficult for us to conceptualize in a highly politicized culture where the "spin rate" on all communications make us wonder if truth ever existed at all. I would define Gospel Truth as "100 percent, ultimate truth." Think of it this way. People may not believe in gravity. They may be convinced it is all an internet hoax or that the science around the concept is all wrong and reject the very notion of it. However, what they believe about gravitational force on the planet earth doesn't really matter. If they jump, they are going to come down. If they let go of a book, it is going to fall—down, not up—every single time. Gravity doesn't care what you think about it. It is truth. Gospel Truth is not "my truth" or "your truth." It is stone cold reality. It doesn't matter what you believe the Gospel to be. The Gospel is what Jesus defines it to be, not what you or I may think or wish it to be. What is the truth about the Gospel? First Corinthians 15 clearly and unambiguously unpacks the concept of the Gospel for us! Let's take a look at what Paul, the greatest evangelist in the history of the world, had to say about the Good News:

> Let me now remind you, dear brothers and sisters, of the Good News I preached to you before. You welcomed it then, and you still stand firm in it. It is this Good News that saves you if you continue to believe the message I told you—unless, of course, you believed something that was never true in the first place.
>
> I passed on to you what was most important and what had also been passed on to me. Christ died for our sins, just as the Scriptures said. He was buried, and he was raised from the dead on the third day, just as the Scriptures said. He was seen by Peter and then by the Twelve.
>
> —*1 Corinthians 15:1-5*

Now let's apply that Gospel Truth to evangelism.

Verse 1. Let me now remind you of the Good News I preached to you before.

Paul is not giving the Corinthian church new material. He is reinforcing truth he has already taught them, and they had already received. Gospel Truth does not change, but our hold on it can certainly drift. *Drift* is a characteristic of a fallen world. For the past several years, Melissa and I have coffee each morning at 6:00 a.m. One morning, I suggested we push it to 7:00 a.m. to get a little extra sleep. She said, "Absolutely not! The second we give back a single minute of our time, it will begin to drift away from us." She is so right! 6:00 becomes 7:00, you miss a day, and then a couple of days, and soon a really healthy and beneficial habit is lost. Paul is reminding the church of the nature of the Gospel because, in a fallen world, you will eventually lose sight of what you allow to drift.

Verse 2. It is this Good News that saves you if you continue to believe.

If you are wondering if this salvation happens in this life or the life to come, I would answer with an emphatic *yes*! What are the conditions of this present/future salvation? We must welcome it, refuse to compromise it, and continue to believe it!

Unless, of course, you believed something that was never true in the first place.

There were teachers in the Corinthian church who taught a message antithetical to the Gospel. They taught that you could have Jesus and still have the things of this world. These false teachers may have sincerely believed in their message, but what they believed was 100 percent wrong. No matter how much you want to believe false teaching or culturally modified Christianity, it still isn't true, and it will never be, regardless of how many people buy into it.

Verse 3. "I passed on to you what was most important."

In the same sense in which salespeople must know their product, evangelism requires a clear and communicable understanding of the Gospel. It is the one thing we must not get wrong. I am consistently surprised at the amount of competition "Jesus came to save us from sin" gets these days for the central message of the Gospel. When a church or tradition loses sight of the need for personal conversation and discipleship, we have forgotten both who and whose we are.

Let's take a look at what Paul said comprises the Good News.

The Gospel of Jesus Christ
• • • • • • • • • • • • • • • • •

Jesus died for our sins. We are sinners. Every single one of us. Modern false teachers out are saying that there is no such thing as sin; if you choose to reject biblical teaching, God must have made you that way. Wrong. Others will tell you people who sin differently than you are far worse sinners than you are, and unless you treat these folks poorly, you are approving of their sin. Wrong. These extremes are both false teachings. The Bible teaches that we are all sinners, and sin is a terminal disease. But here is the Good News. Romans 5:8 reads, "While we were still sinners Christ died for us" (NRSV). We are eternally sick. The life, death, and resurrection of Jesus Christ is the cure.

The Scriptures are an accurate testimony. We can accept Bible teaching or reject it, but we don't get to modify it. God is who the Bible says God is, Jesus is who the Bible says Jesus is, sin is what the Bible says sin is, and the Gospel is what the Bible says the Gospel is. When our understandings and the clear and consistent teachings of the Bible come into conflict, it is we who stand in error.

Jesus was entombed. What seems redundant to us was groundbreaking for Paul. His whole theology was based on the resurrection, and for someone to resurrect, that person had to be completely dead. Jesus was resurrected, not revived or resuscitated. Jesus was certified, stone dead on the cross, taken down, and his lifeless, cold body was wrapped in cloth and buried in a tomb. Jesus wasn't dead(ish). Jesus was straight up dead and buried.

Jesus rose from the dead. One Sunday morning just outside the city gates of Jerusalem, the Holy Spirit filled a dead human corpse, a heart began to beat, God raised Jesus of Nazareth from the dead, and Jesus Christ walked out of that grave!

There were witnesses. The modern idea that Jesus didn't really rise from the dead but remains a great moral teacher is antithetical to the claims of the Gospel itself. If Jesus didn't literally rise from the dead, we have nothing to share but religion. When Paul's letters were written, there were living witnesses who saw Jesus with their own eyes after the resurrection. The fact that Paul feels no need to oversell his point is telling. Paul says, "You don't believe me? Go ask one of them."

This is the Gospel message that comes from the Bible. This is the Good News of Jesus Christ!

Three Questions

Do you know the Gospel as presented in the Bible? Do you believe there is such a thing as sin? Do you believe Jesus willingly died on a cross and literally rose from the dead? Do you believe that because of what Jesus has done, souls can be saved, lives can be restored, and we can live eternally with God?

Do you believe the Gospel? Sometimes God loves on us, and sometimes God shoves on us. Are you willing to lay your bad religion and politics aside and engage in serious study of the Word of God? Can you dare to believe that the life and core values the Bible prescribes offers your best life? Are you willing to submit the way you live your life to the teachings of the Bible?

Are you willing to share the Gospel? If we believe the Gospel, we have really good news to share, and who doesn't want to share good news?

If God Is So Good, Why Are Things So Bad?

Now to take the elephant in the room for a morning walk. You may be wondering, *"If the news is so good, why are things so bad?"* It is a fair question, and no serious evangelist can avoid it. The non believer looks at our broken world and concludes, "If there were a loving and all-powerful God, there would be no evil." The believer looks at the same broken world and concludes, "Were it not for the presence of a loving and all-powerful God, there would be nothing but evil." The clash between mutually exclusive worldviews is something we have to navigate, at times imperfectly, but navigate nonetheless.

My Crack-Free Life
• • • • • • • • • • •

I am not sure how many Mardi Gras Outreaches I have attended with No Greater Love Ministries. My dad founded No Greater Love with the mission of "putting the Gospel in the hands of faithful men." Street ministry was his chosen means to that end. I have attended a few. They sort of run into each other, but some years something stands out. It had to be during my seminary years that we were joined by David Wilkerson's Teen Challenge for an afternoon. They were going to do an outdoor worship service with us, and then we were going to get something to eat before hitting the streets for a night of faith sharing.

The Teen Challenge guys were hard core, not because they were mature Christians with the gift of boldness, but because they had been saved, cleaned up, and off the streets for only about nine minutes. Their service consisted of a group of about fifty men singing in choir fashion (with a blaring and highly distorted music track), followed by a guy who talked about his life on the streets, his addiction to crack cocaine, his conversion, and his freedom from his addiction. Then came the invitation. It was clear that this guy had been trained to share his story with street people. The only invitation he had was deliverance from crack. There was no plan B or varying from the template. The choir began to sing, and the speaker fervently offered his invitation of deliverance: "Someone here is addicted to crack, and God is going to set you free today. Just raise your hand and accept deliverance." The choir sang a few verses, and I was getting hungry, so I began to look around the No Greater Love Ministries team for potential drug addicts. Things did not look promising, and the choir was now out of verses and started verse one all over again. The speaker appealed again to our hearts and informed us the service would not end until someone raised their hand to be delivered. I could smell lunch.

Then it occurred to me, someone was going to have to take one for the team. Looking at the No Greater Love team for potential candidates to simply lift a hand and let this mercifully end seemed no more promising than my search for possible crack addicts. All our guys had their "heads bowed, and their eyes closed" and seemed to be fervently praying for the crack addict among us to reveal himself. The choir was now about 200 verses into the song and the speaker was not about to allow the devil to rob that one member of our rural Midwestern witnessing team the chance for a crack-free life. Supper was now spread out on the tables and stood only twenty-five yards and a closing prayer away. In one of my finest moments of courageous leadership, I slowly lifted my right hand to the joy of the presenter and the relief of the nearly exhausted choir. He said a quick prayer for me, and we all got something to eat.

I can sum that whole encounter up in one word: *Win*. Had there actually been a crack addict in attendance and if they were under conviction, at least they were given a chance to respond.

Though the Teen Challenge guys had only one arrow in their quiver, they certainly weren't afraid to let it fly. You have to give them that! Our call is much the same. It is not enough to know and believe the Good News, we are called by Jesus to share it! And the win is in the sharing, not just in the response of others to it!

The Great Commission
• • • • • • • • • • • • • • •

"But you will receive power when the Holy Spirit comes upon you. And you will be my witnesses, telling people about me everywhere—in Jerusalem, throughout Judea, in Samaria, and to the ends of the earth."

—*Acts 1:8*

The Great Commission is not just the promise of Pentecost; it reveals the primary mission of the infilling of the Holy Spirit. It should not be lost on us that, when the Holy Spirit arrived, the immediate response was to take the Good News of Jesus to the streets rather than stay inside and hold a particularly good worship service.

The Holy Spirit was given to the church to empower them to be witnesses to the person of Jesus Christ. That power is available to us today!

The PING Life
• • • • • • • • •

My concept of evangelism can be summed up by what I call the *PING* Life. A *PING* is a God prompting. We might think of a PING using the acronym of "Power in Noticing God." The PING Life is faithfully hearing and responding to God's promptings. You don't have to over think things, you simply have to hear the prompt and be obedient. It is finding the *current* of the Holy Spirit and putting your raft into the water. How does it work?

Imagine some new neighbors just moved into your neighborhood. Something inside prompts you to introduce yourself, take them a gift of some kind, and hand deliver a brochure inviting them to your church.

I would call this a PING!

PING received. You now have a crisis situation that presents but two options. You can ignore the PING (rendering you a PING-whiffer), or you can act upon it. When we act upon PINGS, we play a vital role in what God is doing in time and space. We may well be just one part of a complex plan.

Imagine this as a backstory. Your new neighbors are Noah and Olivia. They are a young married couple who are expecting their first child. Noah was raised in church but has paid little attention to his faith. Olivia has little faith background at all. Their lives were drastically changed when they discovered they were expecting. This news coincided with a massive promotion from her company and required relocation. Since he works remotely, the move made perfect sense. Now, away from family and friends for the first time, they show up in your neighborhood with a moving van a few houses down the street.

During the move, Noah's mother calls and speaks with them about her desire to have her soon-to-arrive first grandchild raised in church. She reminds her son of the formative role church played in his character development, reminds him of how much more dangerous the world is today, and suggests finding a good church as soon as possible. Upon the conclusion of the call, the couple converse and decide to look into finding a church "once they are all settled in." As they get furniture in place and boxes in the right locations, they are about to take a breather when they hear a knock on the door.

It is you! You have a $50 gift card to a favorite pizza restaurant and an invitation to your church in hand! You politely introduce yourself, hand them the gift card, invite them to church, give them your number, and offer any help they may need as they settle in. As you walk out the door, they look at one another in disbelief with the realization that they have been caught up in a God-thing. What are the chances they visit your church? I would say it is pretty good!

Now imagine that you PING-whiffed. You received the prompt but decided they were too busy for you to drop by, and determined you would follow up another day. Even if you do follow up (which will be less likely each day that passes), a God-window has now closed. What are the chances that young couple finds your church? Substantially less likely at best.

The PING life is a wide-eyed, Spirit-filled worldview where each day is a new adventure in hearing God and obeying God! It is how God uses regular people like you and me to accomplish God's work. The PING life is the essence of personal evangelism!

3

It's Complicated
(Evangelize Anyway)

Jesus was a master teacher. Often, he was direct and clear, but the political climate of his time and the hard hearts of people sometimes necessitated the use of parables. His parables often began with common, day to day things to which everyone could easily relate. Then they took a twist like a major league curve ball. One of the consistent themes of the parables is that they witness to a Kingdom of God that is continually expanding. So many of the stories Jesus told were about things that grow and challenges to things that grow. If we are to be effective evangelists of the Gospel and move people toward the Kingdom of God, there are some intrinsic challenges we are going to have to address.

Wheat and Weeds

Matthew 13 communicates a parable about farming wheat. Since all economies are based upon food and the Palestinian diet was based upon bread, wheat production was a matter of life and death. Throughout Israel in the first century, rural lands were largely owned by absentee Roman citizens, administered by stewards, leased to farmers, and serviced by day laborers who lived on the cusp of economic survival. Farm workers were tied to the land. Land was to them what water is to a fish. The tie was spiritually galvanized because these people worked the land God once promised to their ancestor Abraham. They would live or die with the land.

Here is another story Jesus told: "The Kingdom of Heaven is like a farmer who planted good seed in his field. But that night as the workers slept, his enemy came and planted weeds among the wheat, then slipped away. When the crop began to grow and produce grain, the weeds also grew.

"The farmer's workers went to him and said, 'Sir, the field where you planted that good seed is full of weeds! Where did they come from?'

"'An enemy has done this!' the farmer exclaimed.

"'Should we pull out the weeds?' they asked.

"'No,' he replied, 'you'll uproot the wheat if you do. Let both grow together until the harvest. Then I will tell the harvesters to sort out the weeds, tie them into bundles, and burn them, and to put the wheat in the barn.'" . . .

Then, leaving the crowds outside, Jesus went into the house. His disciples said, "Please explain to us the story of the weeds in the field."

Jesus replied, "The Son of Man is the farmer who plants the good seed. The field is the world, and the good seed represents the people of the Kingdom. The weeds are the people who belong to the evil one. The enemy who planted the weeds among the wheat is the devil. The harvest is the end of the world, and the harvesters are the angels.

"Just as the weeds are sorted out and burned in the fire, so it will be at the end of the world. The Son of Man will send his angels, and they will remove from his Kingdom everything that causes sin and all who do evil. And the angels will throw them into the fiery furnace, where there will be weeping and gnashing of teeth. Then the righteous will shine like the sun in their Father's Kingdom. Anyone with ears to hear should listen and understand!"

—Matthew 13:24-30, 36-43

Verse 24. The Kingdom of Heaven is like a farmer who planted good seed in his field.

Like creation, this parable begins with pure and undefiled things: good farmer, good soil, good seed. The Kingdom of Heaven points to the expanding and bountiful work of God leading to the eventual eradication of sin and the reign of God upon the earth. In his model prayer, Jesus instructed his disciples to pray for the coming of this Kingdom on earth as it already exists in heaven. Whatever and wherever this Kingdom is, Jesus tells us something about it in this parable. Jesus begins with an image that would have been as familiar to his audience as it is to people in the American Midwest today: a wheat field being planted. So far, nothing is out of the ordinary, but Jesus is just beginning.

Verse 25. But as everyone slept, his enemy came and planted weeds among the wheat.

In a very real sense, the Old Testament is a perpetual scrap over the land of Israel. One of the things I have learned during my years in farm country is that farmers fight over land, and sometimes those conflicts can still get ugly. There is a weed in Israel formally called "bearded darnel." In the early stages, it is indistinguishable from young wheat, making it impossible to get the weeds out of the field. This is usually not a major problem unless there is an over abundance of bearded darnel, which there is in this story because the field has been sabotaged. Clearly, the sowing of weed seed is a criminal act, but so is the bearded darnel itself. The Greek word used directly refers to sexual sin, the ancient idea being that darnel is to wheat what sexual sin is to healthy relationships. A weed was an aberration of a proper plant. It looks about the same, but its effects could not be more different.

The other problem was that, because the mature heads of bearded darnel tasted bitter and were mildly poisonous, they had to be separated by hand before grinding the wheat into flour, especially if you didn't want your bread tasting yucky going down and even worse coming back up. This laborious sorting process cut into profit margins, which were already razor thin in the heavily taxed Roman Empire. The saboteur had caused a real problem.

Verses 26-27. The wheat and weeds grew together and finally the servants noticed what had happened.

As expected, the crime went undetected for some time. By the time the farmhands could tell the bearded darnel from the wheat, their root systems had become intertwined. The field hands now have a most troubling report to offer the unsuspecting farmer. "We sir, have been sabotaged!"

Verse 28. An enemy has done it!

Since a statute of ancient Roman law specifically prohibited the malicious spreading of weeds into a field, we can assume that such acts actually occurred. Societies don't make laws offering protections from things that never happen.

Verses 29-30. The farmhands asked, "Shall we pull up the weeds?" The farmer replied, "Let both grow together until the harvest and we will sort it all out then."

The farmer now has a conundrum. If you pull out the weeds, you pull up the wheat. If not, you are either going to have to sort it at harvest or just burn the field at harvest time and hope for better luck next year. He decides to let it all grow together.

"We will burn the weeds in the fire and put wheat in the barn."

This is apparently the end of the public story. Judgment is coming, but it isn't coming now. Everybody had to be thinking, "This isn't a very uplifting ending for a story. The Kingdom of Heaven is like this?"

Verse 36. The disciples said, "Jesus please explain the parable."

When the session was over for the day, the crowd would have dispersed to find food and lodging, and Jesus and his disciples would have slipped away to rest. Now alone, the disciples revealed something we seldom contemplate. They had no idea what point Jesus was trying to make. They asked . . . and Jesus answered.

Verses 37-39. I am the farmer, you are the good seed, the field is the world, the harvesters are angels, the weeds are evil people, the enemy is Satan, and the harvest is the end of the world.

In this teaching, Jesus offered the finer points of a common narrative, which in an apocalyptic Israel they called "The Day of the Lord." God was going to break into history, destroy the bad guys (Romans), restore the good guys (Jews), and the Kingdom would come. The disciples may have loved it but wondered why God wasn't delivering Israel right now.

Verses 40-41. At the judgment I will send angels to remove from my Kingdom every evil thing.

It had to be agonizing to watch the feral darnel and the wheat grow in the field together. We want to shout to God, "Get the weeds out right now or all will be lost!" We see the evil, injustice, greed, abuse, confusion, and corruption and want to cry, "God where are you? Why are you not taking care of all this right now?" But God reminds us, "There will be a day of final judgment; until that day, you just worry about being wheat and let me take care of the weeds."

Verse 42. The evil will be thrown into a fire and burned, and there will be weeping and gnashing of teeth.

The warnings of the Bible don't go away just because no one is preaching on them. There will be a final judgment, and it won't be pretty for those who do not know Christ. Jesus isn't being cruel. God is simply telling us how it is. God is establishing why the Good News is good by illustrating how things will go apart from it.

Too many people want to put words into the mouth of Jesus. They attempt to create Jesus in their own image and then immediately sign him to endorse their products, politics, and social policies. They do not want a savior from sin. They want Jesus to be their lovely spokesmodel. This is something Jesus will not allow. Jesus clearly stated his mission, pursued God's agenda, and talked about the things he thought were most important. He was fearless, countercultural, counterintuitive, and absolutely not for sale! They did not crucify Jesus because he was hypersensitive, never hurt anyone's feelings, and compliant. They did so because he wrecked their sensibilities, crushed their pride, hurt their ears, and exposed their hypocrisy.

If punishing evil were the moral of this parable, this would be an apocalyptic tale, but this is a story of salvation! Yes, Jesus is going to burn the weeds. But this isn't about the weeds. It is about the wheat!

Verse 43. Then the godly will shine like the sun in their Father's Kingdom.

Like the full circle of the Bible itself, this parable ends where it began with pure and undefiled things: good farmer, good land, good seed. When God's justice is unleashed upon the earth, sin is vanquished, the harvest is gathered, and all live in the warmth of God's favor. God's people have good things ahead! That is good news!

The Bible consistently promises the return of Christ. This is a great joy for the godly and the greatest fear of the evil one. The persecuted folks in the New Testament world thought it was going to happen any day and coined the word *Maranatha*. It means, "Come quickly, Lord." I get it. Some days I want to say, "Jesus, the world keeps getting worse; wars are grinding, children are suffering, and division defines even your church. If you are coming back, what in the world are you waiting on?" That is a question this parable answers directly. God is giving us time to evangelize, time to share this wonderful Gospel of Christ before Jesus separates the wheat from the weeds. Perhaps God tarries simply to offer us another week to share our faith with someone we love.

Sharing the Gospel in a world where Satan seems to be running wild can be challenging, even exasperating. Jesus notes in John 10:10, "The thief comes only to steal, and kill and destroy. I came that they may have life, and have it abundantly" (NRSV). It is tough living and serving in a complicated world, especially when people who should have some sense can't tell a weed from a stalk of wheat. But there will come a day when God intervenes.

What do we do in the meantime? We share the Good News of Jesus Christ anywhere we can, anytime we can, and with anyone we can. Perhaps the easiest way to do this in this history of the world is brought to us by a relatively new arrival, the internet.

Reopening the Windows
• • • • • • • • • • • • • • • • •

The first church I served pastorally was the St. James United Methodist Church in Manchester, Georgia. They paid me $11,000 a year. Even at that, they didn't get the world's best deal. The church seated nearly 200 people, but only about forty were left in attendance by the time I arrived. Half were in the choir and sat behind me the entire service. The other half scattered about the sanctuary. I felt like a Shane sandwich. The youngest member not related to me was sixty-six years old. Her name was Sara Ruth Meadows, and for three years, I referred to her as "the youth group." It was difficult to see a future for the church from my vantage point. One day I was talking to a retired mill supervisor named Mr. Ralph about the decline of the church. Mr. Ralph was a unique combination: soft-spoken, approachable, and way smarter than the average bear. He was the kind of guy who, when he talked, people listened: "Shane, I think it all started when we got air conditioning." He had my attention. "Before that, the windows were always open and every Sunday, the entire village sang and worshiped with us whether they ever stepped foot in the church or not. The folks who lived close would sit on their porches. Some folks would drive their cars up close or just stand outside to listen in. When we got air conditioning, we closed the windows and shut the people out. After that, we just started to die off."

While on a recent vacation, I was a part of the online community of Christ Church. One Sunday, I was worshiping from my car when something hit me. I am experiencing worship from hundreds of miles away. Do you know what the livestreaming of worship services has done? It has reopened the windows! Online church can be not only a legitimate faith community; it has also become a place to "stand outside" if you are not quite ready to go in.

Evangelism 099: Social Media
• • • • • • • • • • • • • • • • •

Social media is a perfect example of wheat and weeds growing together. Facebook allows me to keep up with thousands of people at once and offers an opportunity to evangelize as both an individual and a church. There isn't much we can do about the weeds (other than unsubscribe, unfriend, or block), but we can keep sowing good seed. The internet gives us the opportunity to sow a whole lot of it because it is untethered by distance, time, and space. I am a strong advocate of engaging social media for Kingdom purposes. Failing to utilize the internet for Kingdom purposes today would be like Paul failing to utilize Roman transportation, Martin Luther failing to utilize the printing press, or Billy Graham failing to utilize television. Great revivals and movements of God often leverage new technology for Kingdom purposes. Social media is evangelism at a distance, but it beats no evangelism at all. I call it Evangelism 099 because it is one of the least intimidating forms of faith sharing. Here are a few suggestions:

Evangelism 099

Post. If God has done something in your life, like answered a prayer or blessed you unexpectedly, make a quick video, give God praise, and post it! I would keep these to three minutes or so, but tell your faith story. Such testimonies have three parts: your situation, your appeal to God, and God's response. In the time it takes to tell one person your story, you can share it with dozens, perhaps even hundreds. After all, we wouldn't want to make "the rocks cry out" when we can give praise with a quick video post.

Check In. Platforms like Facebook have a *check-in* feature. When you get to church, simply check in. Perhaps attach a photo or short video clip. This lets people who connect with you know that you attend church, where you go to church, and that you are a believer. This can open future faith sharing opportunities.

Invite. Is something special coming up at church like Christmas or Easter? A special concert or performance? A community-wide mission outreach? Bible school or a winter coat drive? Send out a personal invitation to someone likely to be receptive! Not only do you not have to make a face-to-face contact; you don't even have to buy a stamp.

Share. Did your pastor have a great message or a great quotation? Did something inspirational pass your way that moved or inspired you? Share it! Share your church services and invite others to check it out!

Keep Steady. If you are going to use social media evangelistically, be sensitive to the other things you post. If you can't control your impulses or be kind to people who disagree with you politically, the faith-sharing stuff you post isn't going to reach very far.

Things are complicated these days as good and evil grow together. It can be hard to tell what is demonic and what is just stupid. No doubt about it. Let's leverage the platforms readily available to us to share the Good News of Jesus. At the very least, virtual evangelism is a whole lot better than nothing.

4
Completely Out of Hand

A tiny seed was planted in 1987 that changed the trajectory of my life. I was on a bus headed to New Orleans for the annual No Greater Love Ministries Mardi Gras evangelistic outreach. We were somewhere near Memphis when a voice inside my spirit shouted, "Go to seminary!" That was it. No hints about which seminary, how to financially support my young family of four while in seminary, or what I was to do with a seminary degree. Regardless, the prompt was a clear sense that God wanted something specific of me, and I somehow knew that, if I could find the courage to begin the journey, God would guide me the rest of the way.

These were the days before cell phones, so when the next pit stop came around, I called Melissa collect from a pay phone and said, "God has called me to go to seminary. We are going to have to resign from my job, abandon our dreams, uproot our lives, leave our families, sell everything we have and probably take a 70 percent pay cut." She simply replied, "Okay." Melissa is incredible.

Upon my return from New Orleans, I knew I was up against the clock concerning fall enrollment and especially the timeline for applying for scholarships. I applied for seminary admissions, called some district superintendents about a possible student pastorate, and narrowed it down to two schools. By August, we were residing at 16 Johnson Avenue in the Calloway Mill village of Manchester, Georgia. Having no formal training whatsoever, I was suddenly the pastor of the St. James-Manchester Charge. As shared earlier, average attendance at St. James was forty with about half of them behind me in the choir loft. Attendance at Chalybeate Springs ran twelve. Annual salary was $11,000. We were living on faith, hope, and love . . . and student loans. Especially student loans. The people were kind to us, and I learned a lot about ministry during those years.

By the late spring of 1992, I moved our family back to Illinois with a seminary degree in hand and great confidence for no apparent reason. I was appointed to the Sumner/Beulah Charge. Five years later, I was appointed to be the pastor of the recently relocated Christ United Methodist Church in Fairview Heights, Illinois. I was thirty-five years old. At Christ Church, we saw twenty-one years of consecutive growth before experiencing a denominational crisis in 2019 resulting in about 400 people leaving. It hurt. I felt like a veteran pitcher who suffered his first losing season. Then things got worse. We were just beginning to recover when the 2020 global pandemic rendered us unable to offer weekly worship services for three months. We recorded services during the week and aired them online on Sunday mornings. I drove to the church each Sunday and sat in the sanctuary by myself. Then, in 2021, after serving Christ Church for twenty-three years, we disaffiliated from the denomination, and I surrendered my orders. We are now an independent church.

How are things going now? We are experiencing revival in every way!

A tiny seed planted in 1989 has turned into a significant harvest and unleashed a life of ministry Melissa and I could have never imagined. From the moment I heard and accepted the call of God, our lives have been completely out of hand.

The Uncontainable Gospel

Jewish rabbis like Jesus of Nazareth dedicated their lives to connect people to God. They taught in synagogues and instructed their disciples as they traveled. People flocked to hear them when they stopped to teach. Jesus was all of that, plus miracles. Regular people learned from the spoken word because many were illiterate, and parchments and scrolls were expensive and scarce. People first *heard* the Good News long before they *read* it. Some of the things Jesus taught were direct: love the Lord your God with all your heart, soul, and mind, and love your neighbor as yourself. Other topics called for less-direct techniques like parables. Parables were simple stories utilized to teach simple people astounding things. Through parables, Jesus could give his listeners rumors, hints, tastes, echoes, and glimpses into something as incomprehensible as the Kingdom of God. When Jesus opened his mouth and said, "The Kingdom of God is like . . . ," no one knew what would happen next.

In the previous chapter, we learned that the Kingdom of God is like a sabotaged wheat field. Still in Matthew 13, Jesus moves us from the "north forty" to the garden in the backyard. Despite being arid, annual crops are viable in Israel if you know your climate, your soil, and your plants. Droughts aside, farmers have a reasonably good idea of what they are going to get from year to year in terms of yields and prices. You plant the seeds, keep the weeds under control, pray for rain, harvest the crops, sell the crops, pay your help, pay your taxes, and try the whole thing over next year. Perennials are different. They come up on their own and can get completely out of hand.

Annuals stay where you put them. They are domesticated.

Perennials go where they want. They are wild.

The Kingdom of God is wild.

> Here is another illustration Jesus used: "The Kingdom of Heaven is like a mustard seed planted in a field. It is the smallest of all seeds, but it becomes the largest of garden plants; it grows into a tree, and birds come and make nests in its branches."
>
> —Matthew 13:31-32

Verse 31. The Kingdom of Heaven is like a mustard seed planted in a field.

A mustard seed is planted in a field. In my mind, corn and wheat are planted in fields, and vegetables, herbs, and spices are planted in a garden. In biblical times, mustard was a versatile herb that was used to add flavor to food, make oil and medicine, or serve as a condiment when mixed with vinegar. Jewish law forbade an uncontained mustard seed from being planted in a household garden and required it be planted in a field. Why? Mustard plants can get huge and incredibly prolific. No one needs that much mustard!

After seminary, we moved to Sumner, Illinois. We lived in a historic Victorian home, and Melissa planted a garden. One year, we planted way too many tomatoes. I must have forgotten that I don't like tomatoes. I like ketchup, salsa, and red sauce, but raw tomatoes don't do it for me. When harvest time came, we had gazillions of tomatoes, and since everyone else in Sumner had a garden, there wasn't anyone to give them to. Desperate, I went to the grocery store and bought dozens of packets of spices to make *homemade* salsa and spaghetti sauce. For days, I stood in our garage, cooked down tomatoes, mixed the ingredients, let them simmer, and poured them into zip lock bags. We had to buy a deep freeze to contain them all. I don't remember ever planting tomatoes again. Why? The whole thing got out of hand.

Jesus opens this parable in a perfectly proper way. Now comes the twist.

Verse 32. Mustard is the smallest of all seeds, but it becomes the largest of garden plants.

"Small as a mustard seed" was a popular axiom for small beginnings that could lead to great outcomes in Jesus' time. Jesus began his ministry with twelve garden-variety men. Nobodies. Most were from the Galilee fishing docks. Overall, Jesus had a couple of middle management professionals, a political agitator, and a turncoat tax collector; there was no one in the lot to get excited about. Yet, within a hundred years, tens of thousands of disciples of Jesus were located everywhere in the Roman Empire. What happened? Evangelism! It was a mustard seed kind of thing. And now comes the parabolic twist. The text says, "garden plant" after informing us the mustard was planted in a field. It appears the mustard was so prolific it made its way into the garden. Uncontained mustard plants will take over a garden in about a day and a half.

It grows into a tree where birds can come and find shelter in its branches.
No one wants huge mustard plants in their gardens. You may want a few small ones but not an infestation of overgrown and rapidly expanding bushes. Overachieving mustard plants could grow to thirty feet around and over ten feet high and would often be infested by multitudes of birds who fed on the little black seeds. Lots and lots of birds in the garden are not a good thing. They pluck up seeds, damage desired plants and vegetables, and they poop on stuff. Terrible.

And with that, the lesson ended. The listener had to be thinking, "So Jesus, the Kingdom of Heaven is like that, huh?" Jesus does not explain this parable, but he has given us a lens for interpretation from the parable of the Wheat and Weeds. We can safely think of the mustard seed as the Gospel, the plant proper as the church birthed by the Gospel, the field as the world, the garden as religion, and the birds as evil people.

The seed that became Judaism was planted the moment God made a promise to Abraham. Over the centuries, the tiny seed of belief we call faith grew into a unique garden filled with rules and regulations at every turn. But in time, the letter of the law displaced the spirit of the law, and religion turned legalistic, cold, and mean. Then the seed of baby Jesus in Bethlehem brought something new to the earth, not to destroy the law but to fulfill it. And all of a sudden, the Gospel got some serious wheels. The "Big C" church of Jesus Christ was formally born on Pentecost when the Holy Spirit invaded the meeting space of the only 120 Jesus believers in the world. A mustard seed. From there, Christianity jumped from the confines of Israel and Judaism and spread across the Roman Empire. Nurtured by the ministries of evangelists like Paul, Apollos, Aquilla and Pricilla, Lydia, Luke, Timothy, and others, churches began to pop up all along the Mediterranean from Asia Minor to Europe to Africa. Christianity was completely out of hand.

We know from the Pastoral Letters of the New Testament that the emerging movement suffered internal threats and external persecution, but the birds just couldn't get the mustard out of the garden! Every bird Satan sent to hinder, harass, and halt the movement inversely served to spread the seeds even further. The whole of the attack on the early church backfired. Persecution caused the Gospel to spread, false teaching caused theology to be clarified, and incarceration caused Paul and others to write. Right when you would think the church would collapse beneath its own weight, it became more bold and even more focused on mission. The more persecuted the early church, the more resolve of its leaders and more passionate its members. Every weapon formed against the Gospel made it leaner, clearer, more focused, and stronger.

A Midwestern Mustard Seed

Sometimes we read the biblical narratives and are blown away by what God did. But that was then, right? That was back when God moved bigger, bolder, and better than God moves now. Right? Mustard-seed kinds of things don't happen like that anymore and especially not to people like you and me. Or do they?

A Midwestern church was planted in an emerging community in the middle of the last century. It grew to a couple of hundred members over the next few decades and stalled, as most churches do. Everything was most proper. Then something changed. For whatever reason, a seed was planted, and the members began to talk about relocating from a congested retail space to some land along a new parkway about to be built. Ignoring the counsel of denominational experts who advised staying in the garden, they dug up the church, transplanted it to a field (literally), and rooted it in some really good ground. Then, like a mustard plant, the church grew bigger than anyone ever imagined. Then it grew larger still. Tough decisions had to be made all along the way that presented all kinds of challenges, and yet with every test, every trial, and every obstacle, the church stayed on mission and kept on multiplying. Fifty years after a mustard seed was first planted, things were suddenly completely out of hand.

What has become of this church?

Christ Church is in decade three of a Holy Spirit revival with no end in sight! We keep growing, one mustard seed at a time. When you add on the potential for taking our online ministries to the next level, evangelistic reach suddenly seems limitless. With every evangelistic invitation, another mustard seed is planted for God to bless and multiply.

Great Things Begin as Small Things

Great things begin as small things, and small things began with something, even something as small as a mustard seed!

Jesus said, "For truly I say to you, if you have faith the size of a mustard seed, you will say to this mountain, 'Move from here to there,' and it will move; and nothing will be impossible to you" (Matthew 17:20, NRSV).

God is still doing "mustard-seed miracles" in churches, in families, in relationships, and in lives. The question is "Do you want to be a part of what God is doing?" Are you ready for your life to get out of hand in all the ways God wants it out of hand? Are you ready for your church to get out of hand? Do you have the faith to imagine living a life of passion, purpose, peace, and power? Do you have the faith to imagine God could use you as a catalyst for God's work in the world? Why not relocate from the contained garden to the limitless field? Why not embrace a life, a ministry, or a church that is free to grow and expand exponentially and beautifully in love and grace?

This is the choice Jesus leaves us. We can stay in the garden, play it safe, and live a perfectly forgettable life, or we can take our lives to the field, start sowing seed, and see what happens.

Evangelism 101: Gear Up

In the 1990s, churches began buying low quality golf shirts and ironing their local church or denominational logo on them. It was a great idea. At Christ Church, we still produce a lot of *gear* and offer wearables in varying quality and price ranges. We sell them at reasonable prices, invest profits into the mission of the church, and stay up to date each season concerning material, style, and colors. The evangelistic upside is that when you "gear up," people will approach you about your church, and all you have to do is be prepared to respond. We aid our folks in their response by making business-sized cards available that list contact information, social media sites, and service times. The play is simple. Wear the clothing or use the gear, and when people ask about it, give them a card and invite them to church. Brilliant!

One fall day a few years back, I was enjoying a day off, and lunch time came around. Being the big spender I am, I offered to take Melissa to the café of Sam's Wholesale Club. After making sure I had $6 to cover both our pizza specials, we were off. I was wearing a gray, hooded sweatshirt with our Christ Church logo on front and my favorite St. Louis Cardinals hat. When it came my time to order, the cashier looked at my shirt and asked, "Is Christ Church the church on the Parkway?" I responded to the affirmative. "The big one?" I nodded. She then informed me that she had been considering attending a service there, and she asked what I thought of the church. I said, "I like it," and handed her the card from my wallet that offered our website and Facebook sites and service times. That was it. A couple of weeks later, she visited. After the service, she stopped me in the entry area. Laughing, she said, "Why didn't you tell me you were the pastor of this church?" I smiled and said, "I didn't think it mattered, but I am sure glad you are here." She began attending regularly and later became a member of our congregation.

Step One: Gear Up

Have your church order some *gear* at the quality level that most people in your congregation wear. If they won't, you order it and get it customized. Gear could include golf shirts, T-shirts, hats, zip ups, and jackets. It may also include decals that can be put on cars. Don't be afraid to spend a little bit of money; they won't be effective if no one displays, buys, or wears them. Make your gear available to the congregation and encourage them to wear it!

If this isn't an option, order some Jesus gear that has the right look and message for you.

Step Two: Get Carded

Produce some business-sized cards with your church's information and give some of them to everyone. You can also produce a business card with steps to receiving Christ on the front and what to do next on the back. Have them keep the cards on their person.

Step Three: Run the Offense

Respond to any inquiries about your gear by handing the person inquiring a card. I am consistently surprised by how many people ask about my Christ Church gear. "Here is some information" is an easy response to an inquiry. Striking up a conversation is even better!

Step Four: Pray

Once the conversation is completed, have a silent prayer that God touches that person's life and that things get out of hand for them in all the best ways!

Step Five: Preach the Gospel

Too many churches mistake bad marketing for failed evangelism. Marketing is getting people to attend your church. Evangelism is sharing the Gospel of Jesus Christ. They are not one and the same, but they can be an effective combination. If your evangelistic strategy is to invite people to church, you need to make sure the Gospel is preached early and often, and that there are regular times for formal response. When someone responds, make sure someone is there to pray with them.

And yes, the Kingdom of God is like that . . .

5
Transformed and Transforming

The first thing you have to do with a parable is determine if it is designed to love on you or shove on you or do a little bit of both. This one seems more like a lover than a shover. Though leaven is sometimes used negatively as something feral or unnatural, this is a story about making bread. Having the resources to make bread in an occupied culture is always a good thing. You get to eat that day.

> Jesus also used this illustration: "The Kingdom of Heaven is like the yeast a woman used in making bread. Even though she put only a little yeast in three measures of flour, it permeated every part of the dough."
>
> —*Matthew 13: 33*

Friendship Bread Gone Wild

Somewhere around 1993, I took my first bite of Amish Friendship Bread! It was still hot, and there was a sugar glaze on the top. It was amazing. When the folks who gave it to us heard how much I liked it, they gave us a *starter*. What I was angling for was another loaf of bread. What they gave us was closer to a pet. Amish Friendship Bread is not a food. It is a life form. It is like getting two rabbits and one cage as a gift. It takes ten full days to start a batch. Once it is started, it multiplies at a rate unthinkable as long as you feed it with a pinch of sugar every couple of days. The *friendship* idea is that you make a batch, put it into three containers, give two away to friends, and keep one for yourself. It is truly a lovely idea . . . if you are Amish. The problem with us non-Amish folks is that, after a while, you run out of friends and the batter keeps growing.

It was vacation time, and we just couldn't make enough friends quickly enough to get rid of the nine starters of Amish Friendship Bread we had before us. It was time to go on vacation, and not knowing what to do, Melissa took the nine small containers with us in diminutive Tupperware containers housed in a box. In the humid heat of August we headed the station wagon south toward Atlanta to reconnect with special people from our seminary days. One afternoon, after a several-hour venture downtown, we returned to the "hotter than six kinds of smoke" interior of our vehicle. There we witnessed something truly awful. The heat had apparently exacerbated the multiplication process and the nine starters had built up gas, blew the Tupperware lids off the containers and all the batter had left their respective containers and oozed into every crevice the car featured. The odor of dying yeasty dough was overwhelming, and the clean-up job was simply impossible. We rode for months in our yeasty car of death with the windows down. I have never had a single craving for a piece of Amish Friendship Bread since that time.

Verse 33. The Kingdom of Heaven is like yeast used by a woman baking bread.

First-century Jews made their own bread. Though you could doctor it up, all you needed was water, flour, and leaven or yeast. *Leaven* was an unbaked, fermented part of the last batch of dough that is mixed in with a new batch. The leaven must completely permeate the dough, or the bread won't rise, and bread doesn't knead itself. Yeast or leaven was a two-edged sword. Adding leaven to dough makes bread yummy, fluffy, and appetizing. It is the bread of people with stable lives who live in stable homes and are protected by stable governments. It also has a really short shelf life. In much of ancient Jewish life, unleavened bread is called for because it doesn't mold. Unleavened bread does not taste very good, but you can flee Egypt, survive a military campaign, wait out a siege, or cross a desert with it. Unleavened bread is the staple of nomads, soldiers in the field, sojourners, and pilgrims. Yeast is the luxury of stable people in stable times.

She uses three measures of flour.

She has about a bushel of flour, so this is a commercial exercise. The batch of bread would feed about one hundred people. One nuclear family couldn't eat that much yeasty bread before it got moldy. What is baked in her kitchen will bring life to many. She is also a bit herculean. A single person kneading that much dough would undergo a physically exhausting exercise. That bread would be full of water, flour, love, and "elbow grease."

The yeast permeates every part of the dough.

In a ritually pure culture like ancient Israel, yeast is theologically problematic, because it is a feral substance to the fresh batch of dough. In the Bible, it is normally used as a metaphor for the decay and corruption of human nature. Even Jesus said, "Beware of the yeast of the Pharisees" (Matthew 16:6). Yeast was practically good but metaphorically bad. Here Jesus asks the listener to reinterpret it! The listener is also reminded that leaven comes out of dough, a previous batch to be sure, but it was once dough, and now it is both dough and something else. One thing is for sure, leaven permeates the flour, multiplies the dough, and once baked, it expands even more.

It is also of note that you couldn't burn blood, honey, or leaven as sacrifices on the altar of the Temple in Jerusalem; for each of these that were considered to be living. Only dead things could be sacrificed. Jesus suggests that a new life force has arrived. Things are rising, and something new is in the making. Resurrection! The leaven that originally comes from one batch of dough becomes alien to another batch and then transforms the dough into something unleavened dough could never dream of becoming! Jesus is saying, "The kingdom of God is like that!"

Since Jesus does not offer an interpretation key, we are left to interpret for our ourselves. What we do know is that it immediately follows the parable of the Mustard Seed in both Matthew and in Luke, suggesting the two parables were often used in tandem. While both parables are about the transforming nature of the Gospel, the parable of the Mustard Seed illustrates the outward growth of the Kingdom, and this parable the expansive inward growth of the individual Christian. Are you flat, stale, and dry or are you fluffy, fresh, and tasty? If Jesus is the leaven and our lives are the dough, this parable points to one big theme: for Jesus' work to be accomplished in us, he must permeate our very being.

Smelling Like a Subway

I like going to Subway for a rotisserie chicken or a meatball sub, but I don't go very often because, when I leave, I still smell like Subway. The smell of the bread sticks to me, and though bread smells great, it is not coincidence that there is no cologne called, "Yeasty Dough for Men." There is nothing transforming without internalization. A lot of people come to church to smell the passion, peace, power, and purpose wafting about, but all they do is get a nice whiff that begins to wear off the moment they leave the building. The faith may impact them a bit from the outside in, but true transformation happens from the inside out. It should not be lost on us that communion is a formal partaking of the body and blood of Christ. We don't rub the bread on our arms and dump the wine on our heads. We "eat and drink." We internalize, and what we internalize transforms us like permeating yeast transforms dough. When we ask Jesus into our lives and begin to draw the Gospel into our very being, we submit ourselves to the reign and rule of God as revealed in Scripture. We grow in the love of God and neighbor. And we begin to truly transform. Sitting in church won't make you a Christian any more than sitting in Subway will make you a sandwich. You may, however, smell like one.

Four Transforming Questions

1. **Have you internalized the Gospel?** Head knowledge and heart knowledge are very different things. We must both believe and receive!

2. **Are you working hard at your faith?** There is a growth element to a biblical understanding of faith. I wonder if we sometimes mistake maturity for stagnation. Have you been a Christian for ten years or for one year, ten times?

3. **Are you being transformed?** We should celebrate those times in our lives when it is undeniable that Christ is working in us! Let me illustrate. Imagine you struggle with road rage. You are leaving church, and as you pull onto the highway, someone looking at their phone is veering your direction in their SUV. You blast your horn, say four bad words, and flip them off. Any Jesus you may have received has now formally checked out. Now imagine that same scenario happens a year later. You have been attending church regularly, growing in the Word, and God is moving in your life. When the person veers over, you blast your horn, say only one bad word, and shake your fist at them. HUGE WIN! Perfect response? Not even average, but you, my friend, are making progress. This is empirical evidence that God's work is being done in you. Now go and buy yourself an ice cream with sprinkles to celebrate!

4. **Are you sharing the Gospel with others?** Human beings are natural evangelists. We always have been. We share with others what excites us. It's not something we have to force or contrive, it is something we do effortlessly. The best part of our humanity wants others to share in what gives us fulfillment, joy, or delight. Did you find a great new restaurant or see an incredible movie last weekend? Then, of course, you are going to tell other people about it this week! We are hardwired to want others to experience the good things we have experienced. If they take our advice and visit the restaurant or see the movie and love it, it brings us joy! When our relationship with Jesus is where it should be, we will

naturally and enthusiastically share the Good News with others! And when they receive Christ, we will be filled with joy!

Evangelism 201: Personal Invitation

The most effective technique to get someone to make a move toward Jesus is by offering a personal invitation. Always has been. Invitations and recommendations from people we respect carry weight for all of us. At Christ Church, we don't want to do evangelism for people. We equip them to do evangelism. One of our most effective personal invitation techniques is the "gift before something special" method. Here is how it works. In the weeks preceding back to school, Easter, or Christmas, the church purchases a quantity of gifts that people might like. "Special edition" coffee mugs are perfect. We make sure the mugs are attractive, large, and have a good *feel* to them. Next, we slap our logo on them, put a customized flier in the mug inviting them to something specific, and pop them in a gift bag. We even spring for decorative tissue paper. We might spend $5–$10 on each gift, but each gift is going to be delivered personally. If *slicks* delivered in the newspaper are buckshot, this is a deer slug. A hundred mugs might cost you $500-$1,000 dollars, but I assure you, it will have significantly greater impact than the same amount of money invested in mass mailers.

Before church, we line the altar area with the gift bags, and I instruct people to take only one or two bags and to personally deliver them to someone in their world before next Sunday. We formally pray over them, and congregants come forward to pick them up during our last song. In our experience, many of these personally delivered mugs do result in a visit, if not sooner, then later. In the meantime, every time they see or use that mug, the original invitation is made all over again.

Other effective techniques have included church yard signs during political years and door to door "hang and runs" where a professionally produced flier in a plastic bag is hand delivered throughout the entire neighborhood. The boldest techniques include neighborhood prayer walks on nice Saturday afternoons where invitations to church and personal prayers are freely offered. "We are from Christ Church, and we are praying with people today. Is there anything we can lift up on your behalf?" These offers for prayer are surprisingly well received. A lot of people are hurting these days.

I believe the only unsuccessful personal invitation is an invitation that is not offered. How do people respond? Sometimes people visit the following Sunday. Sometimes they never visit at all. Sometimes it takes much longer. Some years back, a new family showed up at church, quickly became regulars, and got plugged into the life of our congregation. They had lived in our region for years. One day we were chatting about what precipitated their initial visit. They explained that they had received in invitation during one of our door-to-door campaigns. They put the invite on their refrigerator with a magnet. Two years later they finally paid us a visit. Not all seeds take the same time to germinate.

Are you being transformed through obedience to Christ and are you working in the process of transforming others? If you are, the Kingdom of Heaven is like that!

6

Risky Business

Our last three evangelistic parables have been descriptions of the expanding Kingdom of God. We have discovered the Kingdom is like a sabotaged wheat field in which weeds have been sown. Good and evil co exist on the earth but judgment *will* come! We have learned the Kingdom is like a mustard plant that won't stay where you put it. The Gospel is hardwired to expand; obstacles thrown at the church strengthen the core and resolve of the church. We have also learned that, when we are permeated by the Gospel, we are transformed. Now let's explore the Kingdom as an object of such great value that we should gladly sacrifice everything to obtain it.

A few years back, my oldest two grandsons joined the Pokémon craze. I didn't get it. They would constantly talk about Rainbow Rares, Charizards, Skizors, and other ludicrous things. One rainy day, Elijah was showing me about ten bent up and well-handled cards as we walked to the car after school. It looked like a dog had chewed on all of them, eaten them, and tossed them up. He informed me that one of the particularly chewed up cards was worth $300. I told him, "Not a chance." He was going to show me his treasure in rebuttal, but as he did, he dropped all the cards in a mud puddle by the car. I asked, "Are they worth more wet?" He said, "Stop it." For months, I referred to Pokémon cards as the leaves that fell from the lame tree to no effect. The boys still loved them. Then one day I was telling this story to someone who replied, "You collect old baseball cards. Isn't that the same thing?"

It was such a stupid question that I didn't dignify it with a response. Everyone knows that is completely different.

Let me tell you a hidden treasure story that baseball-card collectors call "The Lucky 7 Find." In March 2016, a family was cleaning out the cluttered home of their deceased great-grandparents when they stumbled upon another old, ripped, brown-paper bag. Rather than just tossing the contents in the dumpster, they sorted through them and discovered the bag was filled with paper, letters, and some of the old tobacco baseball cards from 1910 or so. As it turned out, among them were seven T206 Ty Cobb cards. They read on the back, "Ty Cobb – King of the Smoking Tobacco World." No one in the family remembered the great-grandfather being a baseball-card enthusiast, but for whatever reason, when he was a young man, he kept the cigarette cards rather than toss them.

Fast forward a year and a half. The seven Ty Cobb cards were individually sold and fetched $400,000 to $450,000 apiece. The total sale brought about $3 million dollars to the family. Prior to the find, there were only twenty-two known T206 Ty Cobbs in existence. Now there are twenty-nine.

Let's explore two more parables. They are about finding very valuable things.

> "The Kingdom of Heaven is like a treasure that a man discovered hidden in a field. In his excitement, he hid it again and sold everything he owned to get enough money to buy the field.
>
> "Again, the Kingdom of Heaven is like a merchant on the lookout for choice pearls. When he discovered a pearl of great value, he sold everything he owned and bought it!
>
> —*Matthew 13:44-46*

Verse 44. The Kingdom of Heaven is like a treasure found in a field.

Hiding places were the People's Bank of ancient Israel. Thieves, bandits, raiders, and invaders were always around, so you didn't keep your most valuable possessions in plain sight if you wanted to hang on to them. Some forms of wealth like livestock could be moved if an invading army came through, but orchards or fields were exposed. The Bible speaks much of concentrated forms of wealth like jewels, coins, gold, or silver that needed to be concealed to be protected. To do so, people often put their most precious small items in boxes and buried them under the cover of night. Owners knew where valuables were hidden, but potential thieves didn't. That worked great unless something happened to the owner, and absolutely no one knew the location of his or her wealth. In such a case, you might know of a hidden treasure just waiting to be found. The best I can tell, in Jewish law it was finders/keepers on small money issues, but a significant unclaimed treasure belonged to the owner of the field.

The person who found the treasure might have been a traveler passing through and doing a bit of exploring or a laborer digging a well or a grave. He may have found the treasure on a stranger's land or his master's land. Why didn't he do the honest thing and report the treasure to the landowner? We don't know, but he didn't. Why didn't he do the dishonest thing and just take the treasure and keep it? We don't know, but he didn't do that either. The finder of the treasure did nothing to earn it or deserve it. He wasn't even looking for it. Like the great-grandchildren who found the seven Ty Cobb baseball cards, he just stumbled upon good fortune. What he did know was that treasure had the potential to change his life if he could figure out how to obtain it.

The man is full of joy, so he hides it again and sells everything he owns to buy the field.

Concealing something of such great value from the owner seems most unethical, but Jesus' parables often had a hint of scandal. And he doesn't steal it; he just puts it back where he found it. Whatever he is, he is not a thief. He also isn't positive the treasure doesn't belong to someone still living. That was highly possible. When he leaves the scene of the discovery, nothing has changed, but everything has shifted. He knows the treasure exists and exactly where it is hidden. His only play is to attempt to buy the property, but that is risky as well. It is going to cost him everything, and the return is not guaranteed. What if the true owner removes the treasure before the sale? What if someone else makes the same discovery before the land is his? Then he has just liquidated his assets to buy a field he really didn't want. On one hand, this could turn out bad. On the other hand, where some treasure is buried, there could be more. This could turn out even better than he thinks. It is an "all or nothing" risk that he decides to take. It is the kind of risk that defines a life.

Jesus said, "The kingdom of heaven is like that" and jumped into a second story without taking a breath.

Verses 45-46. The Kingdom of Heaven is like a pearl merchant who finds a pearl of great price and sells all he owns to acquire it.

There was nothing in Jesus' day more valuable and prized than a pearl. Pearls are formed by a piece of sand that becomes an irritant to an oyster or, in rarer cases, a clam. The secretion used to coat the piece of sand becomes the pearl. It would be like kidney stones turning into rubies. There was nothing considered more beautiful or more difficult to obtain in the ancient world. Most pearls in Israel came from the Red Sea region, but upscale merchants shopped the Roman world for a "pearl of great price." Like diamonds in our time or California gold in the 1840s, it was an obsession. Our merchant has a trained eye for pearls. One day, he finds what he has been looking for his whole life! In a risky business move, he liquidates all his assets and buys the single pearl. The audience had to be wondering, "Is that a very smart thing to do? And Jesus responded, "The kingdom of heaven is like that."

A Dizzying Story

I collected baseball cards as a kid and got interested again as a young adult when a buddy opened a card shop. Over the next few years, I bought some nice cards, and then God called me to seminary. I sold all my cards but one in order to rent the U-Haul and buy the gas for the move. It broke my heart. After I had been a pastor for a while, I began to use wedding honorariums to buy back some of the cards I had previously sold. After twenty years in ministry, my collection was more impressive than ever. Sometimes people ask me how many baseball cards I have, and I inform them that they are missing the entire point. My collection is a quality, not quantity, endeavor. Not so long ago, I had too many baseball cards in my collection. I want only about 200 cards, and I want them all displayed. I decided to sell off fifty pretty good cards on eBay. With the proceeds, I bought a bucket-list card, a 1934 Goudey of legendary Cardinal pitcher Dizzy Dean. It was my hidden treasure! My pearl of great price.

And then I lost it. I keep my best baseball cards displayed in different places. One day I couldn't find the card. I didn't know if I had simply misplaced it, if it had been stolen, or if it had just crawled off like Amish Friendship Bread. I had it, and now I didn't. Risk is always involved in the consolidation of assets into one great prize.

Risky Business
● ● ● ● ● ● ● ● ●

These two parables are similar in that they both involve discovering a life-changing treasure that requires ultimate sacrifice and risk to obtain. In these two parables, the treasure is the Gospel of Jesus Christ, and the two men are you and me. An opportunity came before each man that was far better than anything he could hope or imagine. One stumbled into it, and the other was looking for it, but it doesn't really matter. Every dream they ever had and everything they ever owned was represented in that one item. And they both sold everything to obtain it.

You and I were born into a fallen race; sin has marked us all. Once pack fresh, our Pokémon cards fell into a mud puddle. Sin separated us from God, and that separation was both final and eternal. But God's love is relentless, and God was unwilling to leave us in the mess we had made for ourselves. If the Old Testament is the unsuccessful story of us trying to get to God, the New Testament is the successful story of God strapping on skin and coming to us. In the fullness of time, God sent Jesus to be born of a virgin. He lived the life we could never live, died for our sins, is testified to in Scripture, was buried, rose from the dead, and there were witnesses! The whole of human experience and divine interaction was consummated in one man: Jesus Christ. He is the hidden treasure. He is the pearl of great price.

In Christ, the Gospel is available to us whether we stumble into it like a hidden treasure or seek after it like a great pearl. Because of that everything is different. Just seeing the treasure and the pearl changes everything. Suddenly we have the potential for a different ending to our stories than death and eternal destruction. The Gospel of Christ is in front of us, but what must we do to obtain the prize? The Bible is clear: "Believe the Gospel, receive the Gospel and confess the Gospel." Jesus pulled no punches when it came to the cost of discipleship. Jesus said in Luke 14:26, "If you want to be my disciple, you must, by comparison, hate everyone else—your father and mother, wife and children, brothers and sisters—yes, even your own life. Otherwise, you cannot be my disciple." He said to potential followers in Luke 9:58, "Foxes have dens to live in, and birds have nests, but the Son of Man has no place even to lay his head." He said in John 15:18 that the world is going to hate us because the world hates him. The idea that our faith should cost us nothing flies in the face of biblical teaching.

Possessing the Kingdom is an "all or nothing dynamic"; it is found only through Jesus Christ. God put all his eggs in the Jesus basket. We enter the Kingdom by placing our full trust in Christ. We receive by faith that Jesus is who he said he is. We don't get to insure our risk, hedge our bets, diversify our portfolio, or do anything of the sort. We must do quite the opposite. We must give all we have to receive more than we can imagine.

In case you are wondering, I eventually found the Dizzy Dean card, but I have found a prize far greater. My sin is forgiven, and I have been made right with God through the life, death, and resurrection of Jesus Christ! And because I believe it and receive it, I am happy to proclaim it! Here is the good news. You can believe it, receive it, and proclaim it as well!

What is our proclamation? You can trade the life you are living now for a stake in the Kingdom of Heaven. Jesus offers a life of peace, passion, purpose, power, and genuine community. His Kingdom is edgy, risky, and thoroughly countercultural. It will cost you everything. Always has. Always will.

Evangelism 301: Pray on the Spot
● ●

A most effective way to evangelize is to "pray on the spot." This takes a lot of listening, a bit of preparation, and a bit of daring, but it can also be incredibly rewarding.

In my five years as pastor of the Sumner/Beulah Charge, I seldom had time to visit our shut-ins with any regularity. Sumner ran about 250 a Sunday, and Beulah ran about 150. Either congregation should have been a full-time job. When you factored in that the nearest real hospital was an hour and a half away, there was seldom time to do anything but sermon preparation, attend church meetings, and visit shut-ins. It really wasn't as bad as you might think on the shut-in front, because I often ran into them at Wal-Mart, the restaurant at Red Hill State Park, or the Key Market Grocery Store.

One day, our family was at the Key Market, and I saw one of our Sumner shut-ins in the canned goods aisle. She had spotted me first and was hoping to avoid me by looping around the frozen food section and making a getaway while I was in the back of the store. This was unbelievably ambitious for an 88-year-old woman with limited mobility in an 1,800 square-foot grocery store, but she gave it a try. I respected her for it.

Sensing her dubious intentions (and feeling like this could be fun), I sprinted back to the front of the store, looped around, and when she arrived at the frozen foods aisle, I was standing face to face with her. I smiled and asked, "How are you doing today?" She was now in an old-fashioned conundrum. I could see it on her face. She had stated on many occasions that she was too ill to attend church, but here she was standing under her own power (and moving with surprising speed) in the old Key Market. I couldn't wait for her response! She looked down, gathered her wits, took a long breath, and started outlining her maladies for me from the top of her psoriasis-afflicted scalp to the bottom of her corn-infested feet.

When she had talked herself out, I said, "Sister, may I pray for you?" Normally, I would have said, "I'll be praying for you" but not today. We were well beyond that. Too much was invested in this encounter. She responded, "Right here in the frozen food aisle?"

I said, "Yes, ma'am," and didn't wait for an invitation. I did not use the "inside voice" Mom had taught me as a kid but launched into a ten-minute, rather high-volume prayer in which I asked God to heal each of her various illnesses and discomforts by name. I prayed that her mysterious "Sunday Sickness," which prohibited her from worshiping with God's people but allowed her to shop in grocery stores, would be healed and summarily offered various and sundry other petitions for her as I felt led. When I finished, a smiling crowd had gathered, and she was moving toward the door so quickly that she almost forgot to pay. I checked out, got in my car, and thought, "Love it!"

Want to hear "the rest of the story?" Here it comes! Often we have no idea if or how God answers the prayers we offer for people, but this story is an exception. It appears that, in the aftermath of our holy encounter in the frozen food isle, a miracle occurred!

A few weeks later I ran into the same shut-in at the Wal-Mart in Lawrenceville. I caught her eye and yelled across the store, "Great to see you Sister, how are you feeling today?"

She replied with a resounding, "FANTASTIC!" with more energy and life than I had ever encountered from her. She nearly did a dance to prove it! Anyone could see she was healed! The Lord certainly works in mysterious ways.

Yes sir . . . I have been praying on the spot ever since!

How It Works

Praying on the spot works like this. First, you listen. When, in the normal course of your life, someone complains or expresses a need, simply ask if you can pray for them. Not later, but ask if you can pray for them right now! Don't worry if you are not a *good* public prayer; this is not for performance, it is a heartfelt prayer of concern from the heart.

A Prayer of Concern

Loving God,
thank you for my friend.
I am so sorry things are challenging right now.
Please be with them in the way only you can.
In Jesus' strong name,
Amen.

When your prayer with this person is complete, ask them to let you know how things turn out. Better yet, ask about the situation the next time you see them. Everything is different now. You have been used as God's messenger!

7

A Most Dangerous Thing

During the Q&A portion of a conference on church growth, a participant questioned me about the riskiness of the evangelistic suggestions I had made in my presentation. Clearly some of them would cost some money and scare some of his fellow members. I asked if his church was growing, plateaued, or dying. He responded, "Dying." I told him that, in my opinion, the single riskiest thing a dying church can do is to continue to continue their present course. Something needs to change.

A Popping Metaphor!

Popcorn is attractional by nature; it sells itself. When you go to the movie theatre, the popcorn is front and center. They pop it right in front of you, add butter and salt, and put it in a tub. They don't have to hawk popcorn. They just put it where you can find it, and they cook it. The popcorn does the rest. It costs $700, but you get free refills.

I know something about making movie popcorn.

In 1987, the Herrin United Methodist Church got a vision for reaching the young people of their community. They raised some money and built a Family Life Center (which looked remarkably like a gym). I was hired by Rev. LaVon Bayler for my inaugural church job as the Director of Family Life Ministries.

The Family Life Center was a great facility! It featured a carpeted multipurpose gym area, an office, two meeting rooms, a weight room, a kitchen, two bathrooms, a nursery, and the best space of all, the Loft. The glass windows of the upstairs loft overlooked the basketball floor. There was linoleum flooring so people could have pizza, ice cream, or birthday parties in the area. The Loft was a hang out place with a big screen television, good music on tap, and the new, deluxe popcorn popper given to us by the man who owned the movie theater. It was from Bill that I learned to make movie popcorn.

Here was the process. You plugged in the machine, flipped on a couple of heating switches, and dumped the kernels into the kettle. A little (orange, gelatinous, and artery-clogging) coconut oil was added as a spinning agitator bar pushed the kernels around the heating kettle. You could hear the hum of the motor and the movement of the agitator arm as it pushed the tumbling kernels. Soon the oil would begin to sizzle ever louder, a tiny drop of moisture would begin to radiate inside the kernels, and *pop*. Pop, pop, pop, pop! Soon there was a "whole lot of popping going on," and the kettle was running over as white, fluffy popcorn cascaded over the sides. The unmistakable aroma of movie popcorn quickly filled not just the gym but the entire church. I never made a fresh batch of popcorn that didn't draw a crowd of people who "followed their nose" to the Loft. A little salt and some melted butter made it just right.

What could be a better metaphor for the church?

Every Sunday morning, we bring our hard kernels to the heating kettle of worship. We add the oil of the Spirit and are stirred by the power of the Word as it agitates. We sing the songs, pray the prayers, embrace the Word, and feel God's love. And then it happens. Someone pops.

Pop! A man who has been sitting in the pews for years suddenly gets it!

Pop! A woman who is consumed by bitterness finds the strength to forgive!

Pop! A prodigal son or daughter decides to come home!

Pop! An exploding marriage is put back together!

Pop! A heart is strangely warmed!

Pop! A person is called to vocational ministry!

There is a whole lot of popping going on, and when the church building can't contain these fired up and transformed Christians anymore, they spill out of the church into their homes, workplaces, schools, and streets, and their transformed lives draw the community like the smell of a fresh batch of popcorn draws customers to a concession stand.

Popcorn doesn't cook itself, but when it is cooked, you don't have to hawk it. People will find their way to you.

What a great metaphor for evangelism!

Spiritual Inertia

There is nothing more threatening to the Kingdom of Heaven than faith at rest. In this section, we will discover why doing nothing with the Gospel is the most dangerous thing you can possibly do.

Jesus was a teacher in a culture where people learned orally. *Faith came by hearing, and hearing by the word of God.* Jesus traveled constantly during his three ministry years in a relatively small space. We would not be far off if we thought of him as a touring band that played both small indoor and large outdoor venues. Jesus taught using different methods, but Jesus primarily told stories. I love stories. I love telling stories, writing stories, reading stories, and hearing stories. The introduction to my 2017 book, *Love God. Love People. Don't Do Dumb Crap.*, extols the power and nature of story:

> This book is, plain and simple, a collection of stories. Stories are to the human experience what songs are to an album or content is to a publication. Stories are the "stuff" that comprise our lives. Stories offer our lives context and color, help us remember, infuse meaning and convey the pain and exhilaration found in the seemingly unremarkable act of day-to-day living.
>
> Stories are the containers into which we pour our lives. Stories allow us to savor memories, mark time and measure growth. Stories are sacred and holy things both birthed from and unfettered by time and space. Through

story we can go places we have never gone, experience things we have never experienced, learn things we have never learned and meet people we have never met. If my stories help connect you with your stories or better yet, to Ultimate Story, then this short book has been a noble enterprise!

Jesus' stories were always about connecting people with God and helping them envision a world under the rule and reign of God.

I was taught the craft of preaching in seminary by the late Dr. Fred Craddock, who was the foremost preaching professor of his era. He was the guy who wrote the books the other preaching professors around the country are still using. I chose Candler School of Theology at Emory University for seminary because I wanted to learn from him. Raised in the Appalachian Mountains and steeped in storytelling tradition, Dr. Craddock was simply brilliant. He would sometimes begin a class with a story, and we would instantly be caught up in it. The first forty-five minutes of class seemed like five minutes, and hearing him was absolutely enthralling. But it was in the last thirty seconds that his genius was revealed. He would finish the story and then offer a simple closing line that suddenly transformed everything. When he walked out of the room, your head was reeling. You couldn't move. I would think, "How does he do that?" Craddock said preachers have to trust the congregation. They are smart. They will put the pieces and applications together on their own. We were taught to slowly build suspense into our stories, resolve them quickly, drop the mic, and then let them figure out what they meant after we were done: "Don't tell them everything, give them something to chew on. Don't flood them; dam up the river and let water flow around the edges. They will know how much water you are holding back." Craddock stories were much more than great stories; they were glimpses of the Kingdom of Heaven! His teaching technique was as close to that of Jesus of Nazareth as anyone I had met before or have met since.

The Kingdom of Heaven is the point of any of the parables of Jesus and the sum of all the parables. In the last chapter, we explored the parables of the Hidden Treasure and the Pearl of Great Price. Both men discovered treasures that had the capacity to change their lives and sold all they owned to obtain them. Jesus clearly demonstrated that the Kingdom of Heaven does not belong to the passive. It belongs to the risk takers. The Romans were right on this one, "Fortune favors the bold." It always has. In the parable from Matthew 25:14-30, that theme is both continued and intensified. Not only are the risk takers rewarded, but those too fearful to risk are cast out.

In first-century Israel, much of the wealth was controlled by Roman citizens who were largely absentee. Their holdings were their own, but they had managers and servants who took care of day-to-day operations. It was assumed that the interests of the master were their interests as well. This parable depicts a most common slice of life in the time of Jesus. A wealthy businessman is getting ready to head out for a trip. Roman roads and safe Mediterranean shipping made extensive travel possible for the wealthy, and this guy was headed west, probably to his home. There is no mention of when he will return.

> "Again, the Kingdom of Heaven can be illustrated by the story of a man going on a long trip. He called together his servants and entrusted his money to them while he was gone. He gave five bags of silver to one, two bags of silver to another, and one bag of silver to the last—dividing it in proportion to their abilities. He then left on his trip.
>
> "The servant who received the five bags of silver began to invest the money and earned five more. The servant with two bags of silver also went to work and earned two more. But the servant who received the one bag of silver dug a hole in the ground and hid the master's money.
>
> "After a long time their master returned from his trip and called them to give an account of how they had used his money. The servant to whom he had entrusted the five bags of silver came forward with five more and said, 'Master, you gave me five bags of silver to invest, and I have earned five more.'
>
> "The master was full of praise. 'Well done, my good and faithful servant. You have been faithful in handling this small amount, so now I will give you many more responsibilities. Let's celebrate together!'

"The servant who had received the two bags of silver came forward and said, 'Master, you gave me two bags of silver to invest, and I have earned two more.'

"The master said, 'Well done, my good and faithful servant. You have been faithful in handling this small amount, so now I will give you many more responsibilities. Let's celebrate together!'

"Then the servant with the one bag of silver came and said, 'Master, I knew you were a harsh man, harvesting crops you didn't plant and gathering crops you didn't cultivate. I was afraid I would lose your money, so I hid it in the earth. Look, here is your money back.'

"But the master replied, 'You wicked and lazy servant! If you knew I harvested crops I didn't plant and gathered crops I didn't cultivate, why didn't you deposit my money in the bank? At least I could have gotten some interest on it.'

"Then he ordered, 'Take the money from this servant, and give it to the one with the ten bags of silver. To those who use well what they are given, even more will be given, and they will have an abundance. But from those who do nothing, even what little they have will be taken away. Now throw this useless servant into outer darkness, where there will be weeping and gnashing of the teeth.'

—Matthew 25:14-30

Verse 14. The Kingdom of Heaven is like a man going on a trip and leaving money with his servants to invest while he was gone.

Dr. Craddock taught us the first thing you do in a parable is find yourself in the story. Almost no one listening to Jesus could have related to the man going on the trip. His crowd did not consist of the wealthy or the Roman landowners. His crowd was connecting to the servants. The servants are serving as instruments of the master's will and stewards of their master's resources. They are simply instructed to grow what they have been given by investing it. So given the reality of Jesus' audience, what happens to the servants, not the master, is the point of the parable.

Verse 15. He gave them each money in proportion to their abilities.

Three servants are given amounts of money based on their previous track record with the master. Those previously successful in smaller dealings were entrusted with more and those unproven were entrusted with less. There is no historical agreement about much money is really being distributed here. The text uses the Greek word *talent* to describe the weight of the silver (or gold) given to the servants. Many historians think a talent was a unit of weight amounting to about seventy-five pounds. There is no way to precisely compare money values from one civilization and culture to another, but a talent would have been a whole lot of money.

Verses 16-17. The two servants who were given the most money doubled it.

Loaning at interest was the safest and the cleanest ways to make money in the Roman Empire. Historians tell us the interest rate was about 12 percent annually. It would take six years to double your money at that rate. Riskier loans could potentially earn you more, but you could also lose some or all of your money. The most lucrative practice of all was loaning money to moneychangers. These brokers, then as now, converted currency people bring with them into currency people can actually use in a given location. It wasn't that hard to make money in the cash-poor Roman Empire if you had money. In these first two cases, the master's confidence was rewarded. Both servants doubled their master's money. Outstanding!

Verse 18. But the servant receiving the least buried his money in the ground.

As we learned in the prior section, burying concentrated wealth like gold or silver was a very common practice. The master would probably have done with his money had he not entrusted his servants to invest it. The problem is that this servant didn't understand the master's orders. He was not ordered to protect the principle; he was ordered to make a profit. I assure you that both the five-bag and the two-bag servants had once been in this position, but what they saw as an opportunity, this servant saw as either overwhelming or uninteresting. As juxtaposed to the men who sold everything they had in order to possess the Kingdom, or the two servants who took risks to make more money, this servant played it safe. They were playing to win; this servant played not to lose. It seems a safe play. Or is it?

Verse 19. After a long time the master returned.

Transportation by sailing ship anywhere in the Mediterranean Sea from the remote eastern province of Israel brought uncertainty. The winds might be fair or foul, you might run into a storm; if you had to winter somewhere, a trip could take months longer than expected. Not only that, but people had to carry their money with them when they traveled, so murders of wealthy people happened, and some people never returned home. When we leave for an international trip, we get frustrated if our arrival is even a few hours off, but in antiquity, there were just too many variables to predict when you were going to return from a long trip. No one had any idea if or when the master was going to return home in this story, but there was absolute certainty that, if he did return home, there would be an accounting. Now the master has come home. This is judgment day. The first thing he says is, "Boys, let's see what you've got!"

Verses 20-23. The first two servants doubled the master's money and were praised, promised more to invest in the future, and invited to celebrate.

Do you ever notice that you are excited about evaluation time at work if you are meeting and exceeding goals? The effective servants are about to be acknowledged and rewarded. They are praised, promised more responsibility in the future (promoted), and invited to celebrate with the master. These servants have found favor in the eyes of their master because they have done their jobs. They were asked to grow what was entrusted to them, and they grew it. "Well done good and faithful servants!" Heaven is living in the master's favor and being where the master is.

7

Verses 24-25. The final servant returned the money.

There is no debate here that the master is a tough guy for whom to work. He does not seem overly nurturing. His standards are high, and he demands results. He could be, because unemployment was rampant, and any worker could easily be replaced. Intimidated by all this, the one-bag of silver servant decided that he was going to unilaterally redefine success from growing the money to not losing it. A safe play. A lot of people in Jesus' crowd, just ordinary folks mind you, had some sympathy for this servant. These people were not movers and shakers either. They would have no idea what to do with a bag of silver. The servant was honest about his intent, motives, and actions. He boldly spoke truth about his master; there is no trace of malfeasance, and he didn't lose a cent. No harm, no foul right? And now Jesus delivers the twist that defines his parables.

Verse 26. The master replied, "You wicked and lazy servant."

The crowd had to be stunned as Jesus spoke. This servant wasn't wicked. He was just mediocre. He didn't lose the master anything. He just didn't make the master anything. He was playing it safe and waiting for the nonparticipants to be rewarded. It was his first try at business, and he didn't lose a cent! Surely that is something to build on? Right? Wrong.

Verses 28-29. Take this servant's bag of silver and give it to the servant with ten bags. Those who use what they have been given will be given more. The unfaithful will have what little they have been given taken away.

Now things have gone from a scolding to straight up corporate humiliation. His bag of silver is ceremonially taken from his hands in disgrace and given to the servant the master most trusted to make the most money with it. The rich are getting richer, and the poor are getting poorer. The people had to be about to rise in protest. And then it gets even worse.

Verse 30. Now throw the unfaithful servant out of the house into darkness . . . weeping and gnashing of teeth.

Being thrown out of the house into utter darkness—like the burn pile in the parable of the Wheat and Weeds—is normally a metaphor for hell. The people had to be asking, "Jesus, this is terrible. What did this guy *do* to deserve this fate?" Then Jesus replied to his stunned and angry audience, "And the Kingdom of Heaven is like that!"

Everyone listening had to be sick to their stomachs; the person in the story to whom they most related may or may not have just been sentenced to eternal separation from the master. And just like hearing a Fred Craddock story, Jesus offers nothing else in the way of explanation. He has left much to the listeners, and they will have to chew on this for a while.

An upsetting and scandalous undercurrent flows beneath this parable that pushes on our culturally shaped concepts of justice and injustice. For many, this parable is chock full of injustices. We don't think the master should set such high expectations, but he does. We think everyone should get the same amount of money to invest, but they don't. We think that the servant who buried his money should get another chance, but he doesn't. We think the remaining money should be distributed equally among the other two servants or used to give someone else a chance, but it isn't. We come away somewhat insulted that our sensibilities don't seem to matter at all to the master, and then it hits us; it is precisely these sensibilities Jesus is relentlessly attacking! This parable is a public-service announcement, not a topic for discussion. The master is not asking for our approval or endorsement. And let's face it, nothing more damages the fragile ego of our modern *anthropocentric* theological construct than God being bossy, does it? This is precisely what modern theology fails to understand. The Gospel is not about the servants. It is about the master.

The Kingdom of Heaven—like the hidden treasure and the great pearl or the bags of silver—is offered to each of us, but we have to possess it. It is not enough to just know it is there. We feel for the final servant, and we want to defend him on the grounds that he didn't do anything wrong. He didn't steal the money, lie to the master, or misappropriate the funds. He just played it safe, and yet he is called wicked and lazy and thrown into the street. Jesus teaches us that *doing nothing* with the Gospel is the most dangerous play of all.

The Gospel of Jesus Christ must be received. We don't get it by osmosis. We get it by acting upon it.

Acting upon the Gospel

1. Hear the Gospel.
2. Believe the Gospel.
3. Receive the Gospel.
4. Confess the Gospel.
5. Engage the Gospel.
6. Share the Gospel.

Evangelism 401: Faith Sharing

Yesterday (as of this writing) I walked into Sam's Wholesale Club. There was a long line just inside the entry doors, and I instantly spotted a woman wearing one of our "Love God. Love People. Don't Do Dumb Crap. —Rev. Shane" T-shirts, which came out when the book of the same title was released in 2017. The shirts were popular. The woman, whom I did not know, had apparently struck up a conversation with a woman I did know, and upon entry the latter shouted way too loudly, "We were just talking about you!" Clearly the shirt had brought two strangers together, and some faith conversation was breaking out. The fact that I just happened to walk in had to seem like a God-thing to all three of us. The shirt was a catalyst, but whatever was shared had to be intentional. Faith sharing requires an equipped, authentic, credible, and non judgmental evangelist. If the person with whom you are sharing faith doesn't receive a clear message or can't see Jesus in you, you are not going to get very far. Furthermore, we will never reach someone for Christ if, deep in our hearts, we think we are better than they are. Judgmentalism is like soul garlic. No one need ask if you have some in you, it just seeps through your pores.

I was raised with the "When, Where, and Why" method of sharing your faith story. When did you get saved, where did you get saved, and why did you get saved? I liked this because it gave me a specific time, place, and motive for receiving Christ. As a child, it anchored me. In time, I added *What* to include anything God may presently be doing in our lives. I believe a testimony is greatly enhanced by preparation. These opportunities often occur in quickly opening and closing windows. Every Christian should have a one-minute, three-minute, and ten-minute version of their testimony cued up and ready to go at any time.

Pointers to Sharing Your Testimony

- **Write out your testimony.** Run off some copies and mail them to people in your world who may not know your story.

- **Memorize it.** Clear, concise, and compelling presentations seldom happen "on the fly."

- **Film yourself giving your testimony.**

- **Role play with a friend.**

- **Leverage potential catalysts intentionally.**

- **Look for opportunities to share.**

I don't know of anyone who was *argued* into becoming a Christian. I know lots of people who were compelled into faith by hearing a testimony. Your testimony, like your fingerprints, is uniquely yours. Share it often. Your story is something God can use to reach others for Christ.

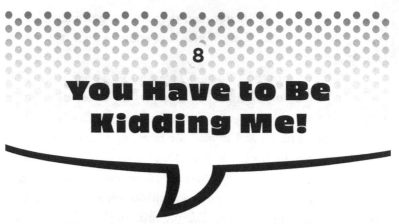

8

You Have to Be Kidding Me!

Parables are far more shocking stories of spiritual disruption than moral plays.

Jesus didn't offer parables to teach folks nice little lessons concerning good manners and deportment. He told parables to blow their minds. Parables are disruptive by design. Additionally, parables are not mutually exclusive from each other. In fact, only when they begin to overlap do we truly begin to get a glimpse of the Kingdom of Heaven. But more about that in chapter 9. Let's continue our soul trek with a most disturbing parable from Matthew 20:1-16.

> "For the Kingdom of Heaven is like the landowner who went out early one morning to hire workers for his vineyard. He agreed to pay the normal daily wage and sent them out to work.
>
> "At nine o'clock in the morning he was passing through the marketplace and saw some people standing around doing nothing. So he hired them, telling them he would pay them whatever was right at the end of the day. So they went to work in the vineyard. At noon and again at three o'clock he did the same thing.
>
> "At five o'clock that afternoon he was in town again and saw some more people standing around. He asked them, 'Why haven't you been working today?'
>
> "They replied, 'Because no one hired us.'
>
> "The landowner told them, 'Then go out and join the others in my vineyard.'

"That evening he told the foreman to call the workers in and pay them, beginning with the last workers first. When those hired at five o'clock were paid, each received a full day's wage. When those hired first came to get their pay, they assumed they would receive more. But they, too, were paid a day's wage. When they received their pay, they protested to the owner, 'Those people worked only one hour, and yet you've paid them just as much as you paid us who worked all day in the scorching heat.'

"He answered one of them, 'Friend, I haven't been unfair! Didn't you agree to work all day for the usual wage? Take your money and go. I wanted to pay this last worker the same as you. Is it against the law for me to do what I want with my money? Should you be jealous because I am kind to others?'

"So those who are last now will be first then, and those who are first will be last."

—Matthew 20:1-16

Verse 1. The Kingdom of Heaven is like an estate owner who went out early to hire workers for his vineyard.

In ancient Israel, the grape harvest was ripe in late September, and the fall rains followed quickly. The harvest was a frantic exercise of "hurry up and wait" until the grapes were ripe and then immediately picking them before the rains made harvest difficult or ruined the grapes entirely. During harvest, a landowner would hire everyone available before the thunder and lightning began to appear in the autumn sky. Planting and harvest were the only times of year when the agribusiness scales tilted away from management and toward labor. During harvest, the master's duties consisted of two things: heading into town to hire day workers and paying workers at the end of the day.

Verse 2. They agreed on the going wage and went to work.

In Israel, men desiring day work would gather in the marketplace during the morning, and potential employers would come and hire them at a market rate. You still see this today in developing countries, and it happened regularly in America during the Great Depression.

An employer in a pinch might come to the market throughout the day to find help from laborers freed up from other jobs who didn't get picked for work earlier. Day laborers lived at the very edge of subsistence. They were desperate. If they did not work today, their family did not eat today. Even if they did work, they had little chance of getting ahead. Their wildest dream would have been to impress the boss and land a full-time job. In the meantime, "Give us this day our daily bread" would have been their prayer. This is a story that Jesus' ragamuffin audience would understand better than most.

Verses 3-5. At nine, noon, and three, he again went out and employed workers promising to treat them right at the end of the day.

The Jewish day is divided into three-hour blocks beginning at 6:00 a.m. and ending at 6:00 p.m. During planning and harvest, it would have been most common for the owner to come into town for the first hiring, and to come back at noon and 3:00 p.m. if more help was needed. Unlike the early morning group, the master did not negotiate payment with the later shifts but told them not to worry about it. Being in a position to demand nothing, the laborers took their chances by working without a contract. They were going to have to trust the master.

Verses 6-7. At 5:00 p.m., he went back into town and hired workers for the last hour of the day.

To go out at 5:00 p.m. and hire workers is to employ them for just one hour, so there must have been storm clouds in the sky to make the owner employ labor in such a way.

Verse 8. He told his foreman to pay the last workers first.

Since these were day workers, they were paid by the day. Those selected for work at 6:00 a.m. would be paid at 6:00 p.m. sharp. It was a twelve-hour workday. Normally speaking, you paid those who had worked the most hours first to let them go home and paid those who had worked the fewest hours last. As payroll was distributed, the workers would get ever-decreasing amounts of money since they had not put in as much time. By choosing to pay the final workers first, the owner in this story has just made a serious business blunder. Suspense would be building now. If the first were paid first and the second paid second, everyone would have gone home happy, regardless of what they were paid. The parabolic twist has already begun.

Verse 9. When the workers who just put in an hour were paid, they received a full day's wage.

There would have been cheering from Jesus' crowd! This is seemingly a parable about irrational generosity. Who doesn't like stories like that? The crowd could only imagine how much money those who had worked longer would receive! Then the 3:00 p.m., noon, and 9:00 a.m. workers also got the full day's wage. Clearly, the generous master had overpaid all these workers, but with each shift, they were overpaid less and less. Finally, only those who had been there twelve hours remained. Whatever the point of this story was going to be, it would be hammered out between them and the master.

Verses 10-11. When the full-day workers also received a full day's wage, they protested.

There was risk in making this protest if you were a day worker. Troublemakers and rabble-rousers were never hired back, and yet the unfairness of what was before them seemed too great to go unchallenged. Their point? "The single-hour workers received a generous wage, and all we got was a fair one. They got extravagant generosity, and all we are getting is pedestrian fairness."

Human nature is fascinating, isn't it? When we get generosity and others get fairness, we think . . . bam! But when others get generosity, and all we get is fairness, it flies in the face of justice. Did you notice that not one of the partial-day laborers complained about being overpaid? People never do.

Verses 13-14. The estate owner replied, "Stop your whining, you were all paid fairly. Take your money and go."

Jesus' audience would not have liked this. They thought the master was going to be hyper-generous to everyone, but he was clearly not going to be. They thought the master should have been sensitive to the labor complaints, but he didn't seem to care at all. They thought the master should at least have explained himself to his employees, but he told them to shut up, take their money, and go. "Beat it."

Verse 15. "I can do as I wish with my money and what is it any business of yours if I am generous?"

Do you know anyone who always has to have the last word? My daughter Lydia and I are both so afflicted, and it caused major problems when she was in high school. Finally, she suggested that, since we both have to have the last word, perhaps, whenever a discussion should be over, we could count to three and then both holler "Ahhhhh," as we walk away. Believe it or not, it worked great! This situation could have used Lydia's advice. The workers were radiating at high frequencies, and the master did not seem content to let things go. Why? There was a bigger lesson here, and he wanted to make sure the "early morning shift" heard it loud and clear. He was mistreating no one. He was simply doing things with his own resources according to his own core values and sensibilities. What he does or doesn't do is none of their business.

Several years back, I was teaching my seven-year-old grandson Maddox to pitch. He was a quick study and had a good arm, but his control was marginal at best. He pitched and I was a combination catcher/umpire. Finally, tired of hearing "ball" after every pitch, he asked if we could switch. We switched gloves, he squatted down behind the plate, and I threw my first ball down the middle. Maddox said, "Ball." I threw another pitch down the middle. "Ball." After about four pitches, I looked at him and said, "You have got to be kidding me. They were all right down the middle. What are you looking for?" He looked at me and sheepishly replied, "If I were you, I would just worry about pitching."

The crowd had to be a bit perplexed. The big idea to this point seems to be that the feelings of workers don't matter. "You are nobodies. Stay in your lane." This was the exact message that the Roman Empire had sent them each and every day. The Kingdom of Heaven is like this? Now Jesus loads up the curveball.

Verse 16. And Jesus said, "Many who are first now will be last and many who are last will be first."

With that final line, the ball breaks sharply over the strike zone. No interpretation offered for this parable, but it is not all that tough to figure out. God is the master, because God is always the master. We are the laborers in the employ of the master. Some are brought in early (the Jews), others are brought in late (the Gentiles), and others even later (Christians). Some will follow Jesus early in life, some in middle age, and others on their deathbeds. The grapes are those who don't know Jesus. To reach them with the Gospel, God needs laborers to make it happen.

This is a story about reaching people while there is still time. God's work needs to be done, and we are the workers employed to make it happen. In the end, everyone will be treated fairly; in our estimation, some will receive more generosity than others. We are just going to have to get over it. This is not about fairness in the workplace. It is about getting in the harvest by any-and-all means necessary. Jesus isn't asking us to approve of it, understand it, or even to like it. He is just stating how it is in the Kingdom of Heaven.

Jesus is saying, "Give yourselves wholly to the work of my Kingdom. Do what the Bible instructs, accept the power God gives you, and give it all you've got. How others are recruited, employed, promoted, treated, honored, or compensated is none of your business. Stay in your lane. Your role is to spread the Gospel."

Evangelism 501
• • • • • • • • • •

No greater joy exists in the life of a Christian than the thrill of leading someone to faith in Jesus Christ! I think of this much like a *closer* in baseball. Many teams have a specialist pitcher they bring in during the ninth inning of close games in which they are in the lead. The pitcher is called a *closer*. His job is to retain the thin lead his team has given him and bring home the win. Up to the point of his late entry, he has made no contribution to the team effort, but suddenly all eyes are on him. When God gives us the honor of *closing* at the point of conversation, a whole history has led the person receiving Christ to this point. A praying grandmother, Bible school as a child, a respected family member, and everyone who has previously shared faith with this person has helped bring them to this moment. You are standing on holy ground, and footprints are all around you. This moment is initiated by a direct question followed by a direct question.

- Have you ever prayed to receive Christ?
- Would you like to pray to receive Christ right now?

If the answers are *yes* and *yes*, I like to quickly summarize the Gospel and have them repeat a Sinner's Prayer with me (see my version of a Sinner's Prayer in chapter 10).

Gospel Summary

God created a perfect world.

Love involves choice.

We chose sin.

Sin corrupted the world.

Sin estranges us from God.

God wants us back.

The Old Testament is messy work of God doing what God had to do to deliver Jesus to us.

Jesus lived a perfect life.

Jesus died for our sin.

Jesus rose from the dead.

Jesus is alive.

We must repent of our sin.

We must receive Jesus.

We must profess our faith.

Conversion is a doorway to discipleship.

Have I mentioned there is no greater joy than personally leading someone to Christ? Whether you have been a soul winner your whole life or are still trying to get your head around evangelism, just being in the employ of the Master is all the reward any of us could want!

9
Stay Awake!

So far, we have explored seven parables of Jesus as recorded in the Gospel of Matthew. Each story is an insight into the ever-expanding Kingdom of God.

The Stuff of Parables

- Parables are not uplifting, affirming, or encouraging. They are designed to challenge every attitude, emotion, and feeling in us that is not congruent with the attitudes, emotions, and feelings of the Kingdom of Heaven.

- Parables do not ask for our consent or approval. They are public service announcements. "This is how it is. Adjust."

- Parables shove on us far more than they love on us.

- Parables treat our sin as a problem to be solved as God would have it, not a tension to be managed as we would have it.

- Parables challenge our anthropocentric theological constructs, hurt our feelings, reorient our thinking, and smash our worldviews.

I came up on the music side of ministry. When Jesus got a hold of me in 1982, Melissa and I formed a band and started playing and sharing our testimonies across Southern Illinois. We named our band El Shaddai because we saw it in the Bible, and it seemed like a cool name for a band. We later learned that *El Shaddai* means "God." Yes, we named our band *God*. Terrible. Back in those days, we did a lot of youth lock-ins where a facility would stuff 200 kids in a gym for an evening and hope to get them all saved or rededicated by sunrise. We would play music and share all night. Then you had to drive home. I remember loading up the huge Peavy speakers and all our gear and setting out toward home, being so tired that I was unable to focus on the road. It seems I always had to drive home. Everyone else would quickly fall asleep. I remember telling myself, "Stay awake. Go to sleep, and everyone in this vehicle is going to wake up dead." Let's explore what it means to "stay awake."

Always remember that Jesus was crucified as a radical. Teachings like the kind we have been exploring hurt people's ears, and they have been ringing in people's ears ever since. Parables are not mutually exclusive to each other. It is only when they begin to overlap that we truly begin to get a glimpse of the Kingdom of Heaven. Think of parables as pieces of a jigsaw puzzle. The finished puzzle is the Kingdom, but you don't get to start with the picture on the box. Only when we start putting pieces together does a picture come into view.

Weddings in the fishing villages and rural towns around ancient Galilee were major social events for the whole community. No one knows exactly how Galilean weddings worked in the era of Jesus (poor people don't keep their own history), but there is a general sense. Sometime after the ceremony proper, there was a long marriage procession led by a wedding drum that led to the location of the wedding feast, with maidens joyfully singing and dancing as they went. People lined the streets to wish them well. Couples stayed at their new homes after the wedding and held open houses for a full week, celebrating and feasting with family and their closest friends. For the fishing and farming families of Galilee, your wedding week was the highlight of your life. Melissa once told me, "Every girl has had a dream wedding in her head since she was a child. It is really 'insert guy here.'" Perhaps things are not that different after all.

"Then the Kingdom of Heaven will be like ten brides-maids who took their lamps and went to meet the bride-groom. Five of them were foolish, and five were wise. The five who were foolish didn't take enough olive oil for their lamps, but the other five were wise enough to take along extra oil. When the bridegroom was delayed, they all be-came drowsy and fell asleep.

"At midnight they were roused by the shout, 'Look, the bridegroom is coming! Come out and meet him!'

"All the bridesmaids got up and prepared their lamps. Then the five foolish ones asked the others, 'Please give us some of your oil because our lamps are going out.'

"But the others replied, 'We don't have enough for all of us. Go to a shop and buy some for yourselves.'

"But while they were gone to buy oil, the bridegroom came. Then those who were ready went in with him to the marriage feast, and the door was locked. Later, when the other five bridesmaids returned, they stood outside, call-ing, 'Lord! Lord! Open the door for us!'

"But he called back, 'Believe me, I don't know you!'

"So you, too, must keep watch! For you do not know the day or hour of my return."

—*Matthew 25:1-13*

Verse 1. Ten bridesmaids took their lamps to meet the bridegroom.

Jesus' parables came from everyday life. The various rituals and customs occurring in this Galilean style wedding would be as com-mon and familiar to Jesus' listeners as our weddings are to us today. The wedding ceremony has concluded, and the wedding party is now waiting for the groom to arrive in one location before processing to the feast in another. This will be an evening procession, and the bridesmaids have oil lamps to lead the way through the darkness. This is going to be impressive!

As with all the parables, things are completely proper to this point. The ten young women have been honored with their status as bridesmaids. Except for the bride and groom, no one is more honored than the young bridesmaids who each dream of their own weddings one day. Their role is to provide energy, singing, and light the way for the procession. It was a big deal.

Verses 2-4. Five were foolish and took no extra oil for the lamps; five were wise and took extra oil.

Foolish means, "a reckless or inconsiderate state of mind." Can I be blunt? It appears the girls were too into the party to remember they still had some responsibilities. The bridesmaids were to take their lamps to a specific location, wait on the bride and groom, and process when the couple arrived.

Ancient lamps were simple. You had a small clay reservoir, a wick, and some olive oil. Lamp preparation and carrying was not a tough assignment, but things did not unfold as planned. Five of the ten bridesmaids had not adequately prepared and had enough oil to last only if everything went right. It was like having just enough gas in your car to get somewhere, assuming everything went perfectly, but then you hit unexpected construction and sat motionless for half an hour. You are going to run out of gas. Wise people think ahead. Wise people have a contingency plan.

Verse 5. The bridegroom was delayed, and they all went to sleep.

Like the parable of the three servants, this parable involves the uncertain arrival of the key character. Night is creeping in, and as the girls were waiting, they fell sleep in the cool night air. As they slept, their lamps continued to burn, so that they would be ready to instantly jump up and process at a moment's notice once the groom arrived.

Verse 6. At midnight, they were awakened with an announcement that the bridegroom was on his way.

It was now too late for a parade. We don't know why the groom was so late, but this changed nothing concerning the responsibilities of the bridesmaids.

Verse 8. The foolish bridesmaids were running out of oil and asked the others to give them some.

Now we see full scale panic. The groom was on his way but five of the girls would not have enough oil to make the full procession. Their lamps would go out on the way. This was a disaster in the making. They would be humiliated; they would humiliate their families and the bride, who entrusted them with this responsibility. They asked the prepared girls for some oil.

Verse 9. They were told to go buy some oil for themselves.

The five prepared girls then invented one of my favorite axioms, "A lack of preparation on your part will *never* precipitate an emergency on my part." Clearly this is not a moral play about sharing or tardiness. The unprepared girls were flatly turned down. If the oil was shared, all the lamps would go out before they arrived at the destination. There was no enabling here.

Remember, it was midnight, and the bridesmaids didn't have convenience stores. What would surely happen is that they would awaken and greatly inconvenience a sleeping family, but it was a risk they were going to have to take. They had to find some oil . . . quick! Now, as though waiting for a plane for six hours and falling asleep only to discover it is leaving in ten minutes at a gate a half mile away, they must shake off sleep and take off in a frantic sprint to find some oil. Now suddenly, they wished the groom would delay even longer.

Verse 10. While they were gone, the bridegroom came, and the five remaining girls conducted their duties and went in for the marriage feast, and the door was locked behind them.

The groom had to be furious to find only five of the ten bridesmaids waiting. I am sure someone tried to defend them or even shift the blame to his tardiness, but it would have been to no avail. You either get things done in this life or you don't. Excuses don't really matter. They all knew the rules and the terms of the deal. Five got it done, and five didn't. The five girls with working lamps lit the parade with singing, dancing, and were honored. They were brought into the house with the bride and the groom. But what about the brides-maids who were out looking for oil?

Verses 11-12. When the foolish maids returned, they asked to be let in, but the groom said he didn't know them.
Even though they missed the parade, failed in their duties, and brought shame to the wedding festivities, they still wanted to attend the wedding feast. People have some nerve. But it was too late. These girls had weeks and months to prepare, and no one was feeling sorry for them. When they knocked at the door, the doorkeeper informed the groom who said he didn't know them. The unprepared were denied admittance. The buzzer has sounded. They were left on the wrong side of the door.

Since everyone could relate to the wedding festivities, Jesus' audience would probably have been split on this one. Those who were always late, unprepared, and disorganized probably were struck by the lack of mercy shown to the girls by the groom. They would have probably blamed the whole thing on the groom. Those who were always early, prepared, and organized thought this the best story they had ever heard.

Verse 13. So stay awake and be prepared, for you don't know when I will return.
This single sentence ties all the parables concerning the Kingdom of God together. It is the last piece of the jigsaw puzzle. Stay awake and be prepared; we don't know when Jesus will return.

What we have learned about the ever-expanding Kingdom of God?
• • • • • • • • • • • • • • • • • • •

We live in a fallen world. We live in a world filled with weeds, seed-eating birds, lazy servants, weak-sauce workers, and unprepared bridesmaids.

Good exists. Despite the abundance of evil, good wheat, prolific mustard seeds, delicious bread, priceless treasures, pearls worth having, excellent employees, delighted workers, good grapes, zero-drama bridesmaids, and happy grooms exist as well.

Good will one day eradicate evil. These go hand in hand. Despite how things look right now, God wins, and Satan loses.

Jesus will return. Jesus consistently pointed to his Second Coming during his short, three years of ministry. The harvest comes, the master returns, the net is retrieved. and the groom arrives. If Jesus said he is coming back, he is coming back.

We are called to carry on Jesus' work until he returns. We live in the theological time between the Ascension and the Second Coming. For this task, we have been equipped by the Holy Spirit to carry on the work and ministry of Jesus. We are to tend the garden, knead the dough, bring in the harvest, invest the money, drag in the nets, and make sure we have plenty of oil.

We don't know when Jesus will return. We have been duly warned that Jesus is coming. This should be no surprise. There will be no excuse.

Judgment is coming. The second coming of Christ will bring judgment. Those who were faithful will inherit the barn, the yeasty bread, the good harvest, the celebration with the master, the good wine from the vineyard, and the joy of the wedding feast. The unfaithful will reap the burn pile, the flapping birds, and the utter darkness. They will be ordered off the property, tossed out of the net, and locked out of the wedding feast.

As we explore these parables of Jesus, the Kingdom of Heaven comes into view and into focus. It is a disruptive and expansive thing. It is the end of time and space as we know it and the ushering in of the rule and reign of Christ. The arrival of the Kingdom is something for which we must be prepared. How do we prepare for the imminent arrival of Christ? Evangelize, evangelize, evangelize.

Preaching Nightmares
· · · · · · · · · · · · · · · ·

When I first started preaching every Sunday in 1989, I began to have recurring nightmares. I was never nervous while awake, but my subconscious must have been a mess. Sometimes I would be preaching in my dream and then suddenly became aware that I didn't have a shirt on. (That would be worse now than it was then.) Sometimes I couldn't find anything to wear before church, and I stood in my closet paralyzed, looking at my clock until church was over. Often my notes completely disappeared from my pulpit as I preached, and sometimes the notes would turn from English into some other language while I was preaching. My solution? Hard work, careful preparation, and getting my reps. By being fully prepared each week, my subconscious anxiety eventually lifted, and the nightmares lifted with them. I still do occasionally see one in dream reruns.

What does it mean to be prepared?

Every "happy ending" in these parables came because people were obedient, awake, and prepared. Every "unhappy ending" came because of disobedience and lack of preparation. We have no idea when Christ is going to return, but we can make sure that, when that day arrives, it will be a good day for as many people as possible. My calling and passion is to do all in my power to make that day a celebration for as many people as possible! If I share the Good News and it is rejected, I can live with that; but to have Jesus return and not have shared my faith is unthinkable. Some people have walked with Jesus since they were children, some are adult converts, and a few are going to just "beat the buzzer." It is all good. We are reminded that every person who comes to Jesus is a Kingdom win, regardless of when they arrive. Our call is to give as many people as possible the opportunity to know the salvation that is available only through the life, death, and resurrection of Jesus Christ!

10

More or Less

The Greek word translated *sin* is a competitive archery term that means to shoot at a target and miss. Sin literally means "to miss the mark." Sin is being anything less than everything we were created to be. In a world that often conceptualizes sin as what we do wrong, this definition reminds us that sin is also what we fail to do right. The old timers called these "sins of commission" and "sins of omission," respectively. I well remember the popular idiom of my childhood religious tradition: "I don't drink, smoke, cuss or chew or hang around with those that do." Might it be that a failure to evangelize could be a sin infinitely more grave than unhealthy habits? You can miss a target high or low, to the right or to the left. You either hit the bullseye or you don't.

Are We "Missing the Mark" Concerning Evangelism?

In 2010, I was named a Distinguished Evangelist of The United Methodist Church by the Foundation for Evangelism. It was a big deal. I recall seeing the list of previous Distinguished Evangelists and noting to a colleague that I was the only person on the list I had never heard of. Christ Church was only running about 1,200 a week in worship back then, but when you grow from 200 to 1,200 in a mainline denomination, attention starts coming your way. Our "secret sauce"? Evangelism. We put out yard signs, printed shirts, went door to door, and taught people how to invite their family, friends, coworkers, and fellow students to church. When they came to church, we treated them really well, offered an experiential worship service, proclaimed the Gospel unapologetically, and offered a time to respond. Many people did. The vast majority of growth in those years were people new to the faith. We saw entire extended families and social networks come to Jesus and find a church home. The energy was off the charts! In the excitement surrounding all this, word somehow reached the Foundation for Evangelism in North Carolina.

This unanticipated honor opened the door to share about practical evangelism with hundreds of pastors and thousands of people. While I was on the road talking about evangelism in churches and conferences during the next decade, I discovered that most churches were badly "missing the mark" concerning evangelism. In fact, many weren't even shooting arrows. They were dutifully conducting worship services each week, but they offered no consistent presentation of the Gospel, no formal invitation to receive Christ, and no place in the formal or informal order of worship for an invitation to be accepted. The churches that did offer a time of response often did so half-heartedly and without vigor or expectation. The majority of these churches were in decline, some precipitously. It seemed that no one other than an occasional confirmand or kid at church camp was receiving Christ, and no new people were becoming a part of their faith community. Pastors and laity seemed genuinely mystified as to why.

My ongoing questions became, "Exactly when, in the rhythm of the life of your church, is the Gospel clearly presented? When would someone the Holy Spirit prompts to become a Christian have that opportunity? What would you do if someone did respond? What is the plan?" In these conversations, I discovered that, in many churches, the presentation, the opportunity for response, and the process for leading someone to Jesus was nonexistent. Somehow, somewhere, the concept of evangelism did not involve directly and compellingly communicating the Gospel of Christ for the purpose of making a life-changing decision. It involved a tepid offer of inclusion into a life of duty, guilt, and obligation. The unstated message was not, "Receive Christ and be transformed," it was, "Attend our church and give us a hand with our stuff. Heaven knows we are tired." Not surprisingly, there were not many takers. I am all for churches doing good things, but the mission of the church is not to do good. It is to connect people with Jesus Christ.

Some time ago, I saw a bumper sticker that read, "Jesus Is Coming. Look Busy." For many churches, busyness is next to godliness, and community involvement is commonly mistaken for evangelism. The biggest misnomer I have found in the past decade is the popular theory that, by inviting the community to do good things with members of the church, new people will come to Christ. This theory was embraced to the delight of the "share the Gospel and if necessary, use words" crowd. Despite optimistic predictions and old-fashioned wishful thinking to the contrary, I have seen exactly zero churches where this was effective in any measurable way as an evangelistic strategy. Christianity does not spread by osmosis. It spreads when people share their faith. The consistent theme of my encounters was that many churches were grinding their ever-depleted and depleting workforce to dust in the relentless pursuit of good and wondering why new Christians are not being made. Many churches today are trying to address their decline by desperately finding more good things to do. The *fix* for any problem is never to do more of what isn't working in the first place. Despite their best efforts, new Christians are not being made, there is no one to disciple, and no one is being sent out to make new Christians. Pastors and lay leadership are getting more discouraged by the minute. No wonder. Churches are getting older, more exhausted, and smaller by the day.

I get calls from pastors and laity expressing concern about the declining state of their churches. When I ask what excites them about their congregation, they almost always open with an enthusiastic list of collective good deeds that have resulted in community impact. Their responses are normally, "We are feeding people, housing people, clothing people, protecting people, and resourcing people!" I celebrate these things with them! But when I ask what concerns they have, it is that they are failing to keep the younger generations, and with every new shut-in, death, or move from the area, the congregation gets ever closer to being unable to sustain their current ministry model. They are dying, because doing good, in and of itself, will not bring people to saving faith in Christ.

Many churches are literally doing good to death. Your congregation may well be one of them.

Many church people are exhausted in the present and rightfully pessimistic concerning the future. You may be one of them.

I constantly remind the people of Christ Church, "Our mission is not to do good; our mission is to connect people with Jesus Christ. That being said, we are going to do a whole lot of good!" If bringing people to Jesus is your mission, a lot of good will get done in the process. If doing good is your mission, your failure to prioritize evangelism will kill you by a thousand papercuts. Doing good without a corresponding sharing of the Gospel "misses the mark." It doesn't make new Christians because it can't.

Doing good works apart from evangelism is . . .

- – an incomplete gospel,

- – a sterile gospel,

- – a gospel of works,

- – an anthropological gospel.

Most churches truly are active. They keep their people busy with mission after mission and event after event without ever stopping to ask if they are busying themselves with the right things. Here are some fair questions for any church to ask of itself:

- – "Are we busy doing the unique work of the church, or have we relegated ourselves to something less?"

- – "Are we seeing people come to faith in Jesus through our mission and outreach efforts, or are we solely a humanitarian enterprise?"

- – "Are we operating in the power of the Holy Spirit to good results or in our own strength to exhaustion?"

- – "Are people coming to faith in Christ and following Jesus into discipleship?"

If we lose faith that God can save and change people, all we have left is doing good. If community impact is your mission, it will become the "tail that wags the dog." If being a valued community institution is your mission, it is all you will ever be. The church is not a charity among charities, a good cause among good causes, or a social club among social clubs. We are the red hot, popping, smelling great, people drawing, Spirit-filled presence of Jesus Christ on the earth.

Let's face it, you don't need a lot of Holy Ghost flying about to pick up trash, drive a nail, work a rummage sale, or flip a pancake. Many Christians have never experienced the power of God because they have never been in the position to need it. To offer physical and financial resources to your community but fail to share the Gospel message misses the mark of the Church of Jesus Christ by a country mile. Let's not settle for making a difference when God has called and empowered us to change the world! Doing good (even great good) does not, in and of itself, produce new Christians. If it did, this would be the Golden Era of the American church. Jesus was clear that our good works offer credibility and witness to the world, but good works can never replace the central role of evangelism in the ministry of the church. Doing good is an effective means toward the ends of connecting people to Jesus, but it must not become an end in itself.

Evangelism Is Not
"Notching Your Bible Case"

Three decades back, Melissa and I participated in a faith-sharing trip over the Fourth of July weekend in St. Louis. Back then, St. Louis hosted a huge downtown event featuring outdoor eats, great concerts, and fireworks shows in the evening. Our evangelism team was eclectic and came from differing churches and faith traditions. Assigned to our group were two young men engaged in a serious competition to see who could lead the most people in a Sinner's Prayer. Their general technique was to offer a Gospel tract, get in people's space, hastily present the Gospel message, and then ask them to repeat a prayer of salvation with them. After each encounter, the excited evangelists would shout to one another, "I got another one!" Melissa and I were . . . well . . . much less successful. It isn't mine to judge the long-term results of the people who prayed the Sinner's Prayer that day, but there is no biblical model for "notch your Bible case" evangelism. If you are unfamiliar with the Sinner's Prayer, it has been used for decades in one variation or another by evangelists in evangelical traditions to lead people to Christ.

I received Christ by praying the Sinner's Prayer. The storyboard of the prayer generally begins with God's love for us, acknowledgment and confession of sin, and inviting Christ into our lives. It is normally followed by a proclamation or profession of faith.

My Version of the Sinner's Prayer

Almighty God, thank you for loving me, and I love you too.
I know I have sinned and ask you to forgive me.
Jesus, come into my life fresh and new.
Make your home in me.
Make me into the person you created me to be.
I pray it in your strong name, Amen!

To conclude, I ask the person to look at me and proclaim, "I am a Christian" to which I respond, "I am a Christian too."

Though I fully realize the Sinner's Prayer does not come as a quotation from the Bible and has come under fire in recent years, I dismiss the critiques for two reasons: (1) The people who don't like it lead no one to Christ, and (2) I have found nothing better to provide an *anchor* conversion story for people. There may well be other ways to launch our Christian lives, but I received Jesus in this way. I still use the Sinner's Prayer to lead seeking people through the doorway of faith. I always will.

What you believe about Christ has everything to do with your enthusiasm (or lack thereof) for evangelism. The lower your Christology, the less emphasis you are going to place on communicating the Gospel. The imperative to share faith weakens exponentially if Jesus is just another item on the salvation salad bar. The New Testament points to an incredibly high Christology, and evangelism flows naturally from it. A succinct conversion statement is offered by Paul in Romans 10:9-10: "if you confess with your mouth that Jesus is Lord and believe in your heart that God raised him from the dead, you will be saved. For one believes with the heart and so is justified, and one confesses with the mouth and so is saved" (NRSV). As simple as this seems, Paul is clear that our faith journey begins with a professed faith. That is the foundation. You can't build a Christian life apart from the foundation of initial conversion.

Innumerable advantages exist to providing a "conversion moment" in the life of a Christian, but evangelism is much more than encouraging someone to repeat a prayer. For Jesus, the call to follow him was an invitation to a life of discipleship. It was not a decision to be made lightly. People who encountered Jesus were *saved* in every imaginable way, and the response to the encounter was "go and sin no more," not to return to "as you were."

The Essence of Evangelism

First and foremost, evangelism is a high-volume enterprise. If you want the Gospel seed to grow, you are going to have to sow a lot of it!

Parable of the Relentless Farmer

Later that same day Jesus left the house and sat beside the lake. A large crowd soon gathered around him, so he got into a boat. Then he sat there and taught as the people stood on the shore. He told many stories in the form of parables, such as this one:

"Listen! A farmer went out to plant some seeds. As he scattered them across his field, some seeds fell on a footpath, and the birds came and ate them. Other seeds fell on shallow soil with underlying rock. The seeds sprouted quickly because the soil was shallow. But the plants soon wilted under the hot sun, and since they didn't have deep roots, they died. Other seeds fell among thorns that grew up and choked out the tender plants. Still other seeds fell on fertile soil, and they produced a crop that was thirty, sixty, and even a hundred times as much as had been planted!

—*Matthew 13:1-8*

In this parable, Jesus establishes that, since evangelism is a high-volume enterprise, seeds need to be sown everywhere. The more seeds sown, the better the returns! It is not our task to decide where the seed is most likely to grow; it is our task to sow indiscriminately. In most churches, not enough seed is sown to have any real chance of a substantial harvest. Here are some thoughts concerning seed sowing in the context of your congregation.

Four Steps to Church Evangelism

Prayer: Prayer is the foundation upon which evangelism is built.

Prepare: What is your bait and how are you going fish?

Improve: It doesn't make much sense to advertise a bad product.

Evangelize: Our call is not to make new Christians (that is what God does). Our call is to spread the Good News. Sow enough seed, and some will grow.

Let's look at these four components individually:

Evangelistic Prayer

Evangelism begins with prayer. Prayer plants dynamite. Evangelism detonates dynamite. You can't detonate what has not been planted.

Action Plan: Gather a prayer team and meet once a week for prayer before your morning worship service. Spend time praising God. Spend time in confession for a lack of passion for evangelism, failing to reach people for Christ, and failing to grow God's church. Thank God for the gift of your congregation, and pray for power in your worship service, an evangelistic spirit, your inactive rolls, the folks God is getting ready to send you, and souls for God's Kingdom. Organize a prayer walk through your community. Pray for the people you see and over the houses and businesses you pass. Go in pairs. Don't be afraid to stop and talk to folks and tell them what you are doing! People will think you are nuts, but you will be God's kind of nuts! Create some buzz.

Evangelistic Preparation

Are you ready to receive the folks you hope come to your church? Are your facilities in tip-top condition? Is your church clean? Do some things need a fresh coat of paint? Are the carpets clean? Is the décor up to date? Are your restrooms comparable to those of local restaurants? Is your sound system a distraction? Is there adequate parking? Do you have greeters at the doors (inside and out)? Is there a welcome center? How will you welcome first time visitors? How will you follow them up within the week?

Action Plan: Plan an "Extreme Church Makeover" as a part of your evangelism program. Get the congregation excited about some Saturday workdays. Investing in a consultant or interior decorator to give you "fresh eyes" will be worth the money that it costs on this one. Have the Trustees make a list of tasks to accomplish. Recruit a "home mission" work team, plan well, start early, and transform your space!

Improve Worship

Focus your resources on improving your Sunday morning worship service. Make it budget priority one! People today respond to culturally relevant music, images, and challenging biblical messages with practical application. They are not looking to track through a bulletin; they are hoping to experience God. Improve your product before you advertise!

Action Plan: Send out a team of spies this summer to visit growing churches of the next size plateau and see what they are do-

ing in worship that you are not. Pastors, attend church growth semi-
nars, preaching conferences, visit a megachurch or two, and listen to
preachers leading growing churches online. Increase your vision and
improve your craft. Musicians: update your look, your music, your
quality, and your attitudes. Plan a major fall kick off the Sunday after
Labor Day with a new message series, some new bells and whistles,
and some new décor. "Grand Re-Opening!" Do the same thing again
at Christmas, and then at Easter.

Invite People to Church

Get on the radar screens of your community. People may
drive by your building every day, but do they know your church is
there? Ask yourself, "Who is my target audience? What do we want
to say to them? What do we want them to do in light of our message?" No money? No problem!

Here are some practical evangelism ideas that have zero budget impact:

1. Create a culture of inviting at your church. It is free to
   invite someone! It has been my observation that it takes
   about twenty invitations to get one visitor. Remember,
   your task is to make the invites; God will handle the
   rest!

2. Take a pie or something to the folks who pay you a visit
   and leave you their information (have people bake them
   on Monday and deliver on Tuesday). Until our church
   ran 400 or so, I delivered these baked goods personally.

3. Use social media by every means possible.

4. Make welcome boxes for your folks to take to new
   residents when people get a new neighbor or coworker.
   Include things like custom pens and a mug, an updated
   brochure, your church Facebook or website, and an
   invitation to worship. Charge your folks for the cost of

the box they will deliver. There is nothing wrong with having some "skin in the game."

5. Yard signs and window decals are a fun way to get out your message. Have some professionally made and charge folks the cost for the pair.

6. Get in the local news every chance you can with exciting and relevant things. Have your best writers write the stories. Take good pictures of actual humans.

7. Leverage things with community interest like food drives, coat drives, relief efforts, and work trips. Invite the community to participate with drop-offs. Hold a consecration service before you send stuff out and invite all donors to attend!

8. Go door to door on a Saturday afternoon and personally invite people to worship. The more contacts you make, the greater impact it will have!

Crazy Gospel Math
• • • • • • • • • • • •

I sometimes get the opportunity to help pastors and congregations think about evangelism and growth. Here is a formula I use to determine realistic goals: take your sanctuary capacity, multiply it by .75, and double it. That is your Sunday morning potential. I see a lot of churches that were constructed to seat about 200, so let's use this as a starting place. Multiplying 200 by 75 percent will give you 150; so double it to get 300. Your building would allow you to comfortably reach 300 people each week in two, high-quality Sunday morning services. I would suggest 9:00 a.m. and 10:30 a.m. as worship times. Doing two identical Sunday services is quite efficient and easily done. Now for the big question: how do you get those additional people to attend? The answer is elementary: you invite them.

Now let's get out our Crazy Gospel Math calculator. I want to suggest that a church with a sanctuary that holds 200 and averages 100 adults in attendance each week can be less than two years away from reaching their building potential of 300. Two years!

In the parable of the Sower, Jesus promises that some of the seeds we sow will fall on receptive hearts and yield a good harvest. Not all of them or most of them but some of them. Imagine that your 100 people decided to offer one invitation to worship to a different person or family every week for the next year. That would be 52 invites per person and a total of 5,200 personal invitations to worship. Now imagine that only one out of the 52 resulted in someone who plugged into your church. Honestly, that one does not even take a whole lot of faith. After one year, your church would be running over 200 each weekend. If those 200 did the same thing and had the same conservative yield of 1 in 52 results, you would be maxed out at 300 in a year and a half.

The key is volume. You have to get 100 living people who attend your church to actually make the invitations. They also need to realize that inviting the same person 100 times, is not 100 invitations; it is one. That is really closer to stalking. It is staggering to think what God could do with 100 people who are willing to risk something as "absolutely doable" as inviting one new person a week to church. If you disagree with the formula or my answer, I invite you to try it yourself and prove me wrong. No downside on this one.

I Like My Way Better
• • • • • • • • • • • •

When I was young, my dad was a Southern Baptist pastor. All seemed to be going well until he got "all Spirit-filled" and began sharing faith with people outside the church. To make matters worse, he began to go to local taverns and talk to people about Jesus. He organized Jesus marches where groups would carry a cross thorough a community, and got Christian rock bands to play music across from high schools. He printed up hundreds of thousands of Big Question tracts, started sharing faith at national events, and befriended the lost. Before long, some church folk got thinking Dad was spending too much time with people who weren't paying his salary and not enough time with the people who were. They felt the pastor's role was to care for the ninety-nine sheep still in the fold, not waste his time searching for the one lost sheep.

Time after time, he was formally confronted by those who claimed his methods of evangelism were not just unorthodox but all wrong. I remember one confrontation with an angry man in the entry way to the church who did not know I was watching. He unloaded on Dad and, to my surprise, Dad just took it . . . and took it . . . and took it. When the man had blown most of the wind from his sails and said his piece, Dad asked, "What are you doing to win people to Christ?"

Dead calm, then, "Nothing."

Dad broke the silence, "I like my way better."

Evangelism can be motivated by any number of things. As a young man, my motivation was often duty. As I get older, my desire to share the Good News is increasingly motived by love. The Holy Spirit has called, equipped, and empowered us to connect lost and hurting people to the God who not only created them but loves them. This is Good News. On June 22, 2009, I became a grandfather for the very first time. A part of the fun was deciding what our new grandchild would call us. Melissa wanted to be called Nana. I chose The Great and Mighty Papa. Both names stuck. By all accounts, being a Papa softened me, and if "Harold" was the defining story of my early ministry years, this account with three of my grandchildren has defined my later years.

Poop-a-geddon
• • • • • • • • •

When Fairview Heights, Illinois got a Chick-fil-A a few years back, it was a game changer for the local fast-food industry. The place was clean, the employees friendly, and if the food wasn't cheap, it was consistent and good. Business was brisk. Back in those days, we lived in the hive of suburbia, and Fridays were normally a full morning and afternoon with my four young grandchildren; Melissa watched all four grandkids each weekday. I used to sleep in every Friday, take the dog for a walk, take a shower, eat some lunch out, and then do nothing for the rest of the day. That was before we had grandchildren. Life was different now.

One Friday, I had planned to take my oldest grandson Maddox to Chick-fil-A. This one-on-one time always goes well, and it gives Melissa a three-to-one ratio with the little ones for a couple of hours. However, I discovered that my grandson Elijah was coming along, and suddenly it didn't seem right to leave granddaughter Mabry at home. In a moment of extreme courage, I determined to take all three of them (ages four, three, and two) to Chick-fil-A . . . alone. I loaded up Melissa's Jeep Commander, installed car seats (two of which are the size of living room recliners), and secured my tribe. I left one-year-old Isaac with Melissa and was feeling pretty good about myself. I was clearly demonstrating servant leadership (this being my day off and all) by taking three children off Melissa's hands for a couple of hours and opening the door for great memories with Papa and some bonding time. In a moment of temporary sanity, I called my dad to see if he wanted to come along, but when he heard I had all three kids, he made up a lame excuse as to why he was not coming. I was on my own.

When I arrived, I set them each free, and we all held hands crossing the parking lot. Things were going so well until I opened the door. I don't know what possessed Elijah, but he immediately ran to the condiment section and began throwing packets of mayonnaise across the serving area. I quickly reprimanded him and placed our orders. Once seated just across from the glass-enclosed play area, I fixed their drinks and prepared their meals. Then Mabry saw Elijah's chocolate milk and suddenly forgot that she had told me two minutes earlier that she wanted lemonade. The second I got her calmed down, I noted Elijah was crushing his round hashbrowns in his hand and had already thrown several under the table at Maddox. I had forgotten napkins, so I scooted to the front (leaving the kids) and grabbed a handful to clean up the tater tots; then I noticed all three children were standing on their seats looking over the divider at me yelling "poop." You have to understand, *poop* is the worst word they know, and they always get in trouble for saying poop, but now all three were yelling "poop" and laughing uncontrollably. Once we had survived lunch (and the "poop-a-geddon"), it was time for the easy part, turning them loose in the glass-enclosed, soundproof, and perfectly safe playland. I ushered them inside and reached into my pocket for my phone to check messages and have some "Shane" time. "Poop, I left my phone in the car." Running for napkins seemed acceptable, but actually leaving the building seemed irresponsible. I thought about asking one of the exceptionally polite workers to run and get my phone and assumed they would have responded, "My pleasure," but that too seemed a stretch. I was going to have to go without a phone.

Then I heard something from the soundproof room. They were screaming, not hurt or mad, just screaming to see how loud they could scream. At this point, I imagined they were someone else's grandchildren (this technique had worked great with my kids), but when I looked up, Maddox and Elijah had climbed on top of the interior door handle and were jumping off. Mabry had somehow managed to abscond with Elijah's chocolate milk, take it into the play area, and spill it all over the floor. It was at this point that I considered locking the play area, calling both sets of parents, informing them their children were locked inside, and leaving. Instead, I went back for more napkins and cleaned up the mess.

Now at my wit's end, I told them we were leaving because they could not obey. They all three ran into the tubular slide where I could hear them laughing and saying "poop." Finally, I coaxed them out, put on their shoes, and got them headed toward the door where we exited, held hands across the parking lot of shame, and reloaded. I started the car and swore we were never going to do this again. Then I looked in the rearview mirror.

They were absolutely . . . beautiful.

Those little disobedient, *poop*-slinging snotwads were absolutely beautiful! They are my descendants, my legacy, my people, and my tribe. I am absolutely crazy about them! Not because they are always good (they were not good), but because they will always be mine.

I think God sees us the same way. We are His creation, His reflection, His people and His tribe.

He is crazy about us!

Not because we are good but because we are His!

Most of Paul's letters were written to churches, but First and Second Timothy were written to Paul's spiritual son Timothy. Paul met Timothy in the middle part of the first century on his Second Missionary Journey that started in AD 49, lasted until AD 52, and spanned more than 2,250 miles. This trip was essentially a "first contact" mission in which Paul took the Gospel to a European continent. Paul saw something in Timothy. Quickly, Timothy became Paul's protégé and later, his most trusted companion. Many years later, Paul wrote to his son in the Lord these legacy words that provide the perfect ending for a book on evangelism.

Instruction Manual—2 Timothy 4:2-5
• •

Verse 2. Preach the word of God. Be prepared, whether the time is favorable or not. Patiently correct, rebuke, and encourage your people with good teaching.

> **Proclaim the word of God**. Give it to them straight. A watered-down Gospel message lacks the firepower to effect spiritual change.

> **Patiently Correct.** This type of patience reflects a spirit that never grows tired or irritated.

> **Rebuke.** A rebuke is an intervention that invariable risks conflict to work toward a greater good. Sometimes you have to love people enough to tell them the truth. It is what you do when patient correction doesn't work.

> **Encourage.** Encouragement must follow rebuke. Otherwise, we tear down but fail to rebuild.

Verses 3-4. For a time is coming when people will no longer listen to sound and wholesome teaching. They will follow their own desires and will look for teachers who will tell them whatever their itching ears want to hear. They will reject the truth and chase after myths.

> **Hold fast to Sound Teaching.** Sound teaching is rooted in Scripture. It is not expedient or pragmatic. It is immutable.

> **Reject False Teaching**. False teaching is rooted in shifting culture and political sensibilities. It is relative.

Verse 5. But you should keep a clear mind in every situation. Don't be afraid of suffering for the Lord and fully carry out the ministry God has given you.

> **Have a clear mind**. Hold steady. Keeping the big goal in mind keeps us from being distracted by smaller things. Our existence in time and space is only the smallest sliver of our life's eternal. The most important decision we will make in this world, concerns the next.

> **Don't be afraid.** Tap into the power of the Holy Spirit.

> **Bring others to Christ**. Sow the seeds and God will take care of growth.

> **Finish strong.** Be faithful until the end of your life or until the return of Christ.

It is impossible to write a comprehensive book on evangelism. I made no attempt to do so. I write from my own experience and report what I have seen with my own eyes and experienced in my own life. If this book has inspired and equipped you to become a more intentional evangelist and has given you an evangelistic idea or two, my reason for writing has been fulfilled! If you reject every idea I have shared and are determined to prove me wrong by being more effective in evangelism than I ever dreamed, that is better still. My way of doing things is not the only way; it is my way. We are not in competition; we are on the same team.

The shift from an inertial, listless church at rest to an evangelistic church in motion requires force. I believe that force comes directly from Jesus Christ. He was a catalyst and called his followers to be catalysts as well. We have good news to share, but to share it, you have to do something . . . anything.

Holding the Sign

When I was in seminary (1989–1992), I was a student pastor at two small churches in Manchester, Georgia. St. James was a mill village church. After a year of accomplishing nothing other than conducting funerals, I couldn't stand it any longer. I was going to do something. I borrowed a huge fifteen-foot sign from my dad that read, "Smile, Jesus Loves You" on one side and "Jesus Heals Broken Hearts" on the other. Then I "set up camp" on the busiest intersection in town on several Saturday nights, leaned on the hood of my vintage 1962 Studebaker Lark, and held the sign. My thinking was that people driving by would read the sign; if someone stopped, I would talk to them about Jesus. That was it. That was the plan.

People must have thought I was crazy, but I didn't know what to do, and doing nothing was not an option. A few people did stop to talk out of curiosity, and I told my story. "I am the pastor of St. James over in the mill village, and since no one is coming our way, I decided to set up here." They smiled, shook their heads, and drove off. After a couple of weeks, a single parishioner named James joined me. James said only about six words a year, so when someone stopped and asked what we were doing, I didn't answer. I just looked at James. I couldn't wait to hear his response. When he saw that answering was going to be up to him, he looked at them as though they were crazy and said in a thick southern drawl, "Holding this sign." When they glanced my way for further explanation, I gave them my best *duh* look.

It occurred to me in that moment, that James and I were "Jesus Activists." We were not activists on behalf of causes we felt Jesus would support or for our brand of politics. We were activists for Jesus himself. We were two flawed men sharing the Good News under the influence of the Holy Spirit. In the simple act of parking our vehicles and hoisting a sign, we put ourselves in a position for God to use us, should God wish to do so. It also occurred to me that this is all God asks.

That's what evangelism is, isn't it? It is intentionally putting yourself in position to be a catalyst God can use to bring others to his son Jesus Christ. You don't have to be exceptional or "slightly irregular" to share your faith; you just have to be willing to hold the sign.

A Closing Prayer
• • • • • • • • • • •

Almighty God,
Thank you for the Good News of the Gospel.
It has changed our lives.
Empower us to boldly and effectively share Jesus with others.
In the Strong Name of Jesus,
Amen!

SCAN HERE to learn more about Invite Press, a premier publishing imprint created to invite people to a deeper faith and living relationship with Jesus Christ.

Printed in the USA
CPSIA information can be obtained
at www.ICGtesting.com
BVHW040755040823
668180BV00004B/20

9 781953 495556